THE REQUIEM
OF A CITY CHURCH

Leonard Urban

Ancient Echoes Publishing Co.
Bellvue, CO 80512-0125

Ancient Echoes Publishing Co.
P.O. Box 125
Bellvue, CO 80512-0125

Design by Maureen Morris

Library of Congress Card Catalog Number: 90-81327

Urban, Leonard
    The Requiem of a City Church
    Look What They've Done to My Church

ISBN 0-9626432-0-3

Dedication

This volume is gratefully dedicated to the parishioners of St. Philomena's Church, every person who set foot inside its doors... for sanctuary and more.

Contents

Preface

There is nothing more delightful and heart warming than a story. One muses that from ancient times stories were passed around and passed on, into the hands and hearts of eager hearers for safekeeping and handing down, and down, embracing generations far beyond original intent.

It is a sadness of life that stories are too often lost, have withered to mere recollections, with no one to keep them alive and well. It is painful just to think that tales of human and heroic endeavor have returned to oblivion forever. Ponder for a moment... some elder, one of the revered sages of the tribe or clan, whose eyes and heart hold careful memories of days past, spinning out some event, entrancing enchanted listeners. What intriguing mystery to the simple words: "Once upon a time..." or, "It happened on one occasion..." How tragic when a good story is lost, with no one to hold it for safekeeping, having to fend for its existence "out there," in the labyrinths of wordless silence. No wonder we take care about them, pass them on.

The inevitable value of any story is simply that it engages us immediately, places us in the center of things, lets us relate. And all that because life is a shared experience, actually not too different for any of us. We are the characters of almost every adventure. If someone in the story is happy, we can say we have been also. Where there is sadness, it is not too difficult a stretch of our fertile imagination to identify and feel. We relish the victory of a hero, and lament the staggering, bleak storm of defeat. Whatever happens in the story happens to me, takes its place there, inside. It becomes mine.

This is the story of a church, perhaps nondescript and unremarkable at first glance. It could be almost any church. There are so many. They all seem somewhat the same, spires and stained glass, pews and holy fixtures, dim light and ominous silence. It is the tale of only one church, whose life is short, as contrasted with the longer view of things.

But the story, like all stories, unfolds to reveal that nothing is ever ordinary, casual. Its characters, a melange of that symphony of players, whose parts fall together into completion and harmony, offer the stuff of what is deeply human. There is no perfection here. Of course not. There is no true story of perfect people. There is only a kind of unconscious and even unintended beauty. Wherever people gather one finds a degree of tension, the heave and sway of existence. It is from such erstwhile mix that grace comes alive, the simple state of disarming bloom. What we thought was rare and unusual are actually common, cutting across our lives and proving our own worth. Every story is a gift, which teaches us who we are, inside, deep down.

To personify a church, give it flesh, a heartbeat, the anxious hope for immortality, is an effort not to let so much life and energy die. It is a longing in all of us. St. Philomena becomes our advocate, speaking our intense yearnings, the wish to stay, even after we have passed beyond what is sensible and concrete. God ought to offer us at least that much, the assurance that we need not leave, fall so quickly into oblivion, be swept too precipitately into the corners of sleep with no waking.

Let St. Philomena tell her story then. It is the story of all of us and leaves room for our own chapter and verse. I hope you find yourself there, not in one, but in all the characters, from Harvard Brophy, to Marigold to Tom and Billy. I hope you will let Willie into your heart, not begrudging his capricious character, the bravura which so aptly covers his gentle spirit. Treat the Assistants kindly, men of good intentions, of whom the Church and theology have asked perhaps too much, sometimes impossible tasks of response and virtue. Welcome, if you will please, those all too human individuals who peopled the pews of that sacred precinct. Ask no more of them than you would of yourself, who struggle and sigh, surmount the hurdles of faith and practice, find God in your own way and end with the hope of peaceful consolation.

Here then is the story, a soft spiration heard faintly over a larger breathing, a sound inside a voiceless silence, a written word which fills a spotless page. It is a simple offering, asking nothing more than to be heard, and told again, this time in your words, to be passed on.

Blessed are the people, the saints, who believe, even the unbelievable, who come and come again, whose lives are written down, in testimonies that life is good, God's gracious gift, to be seen and heard and never forgotten.

Chapter One

THE LAST SIGHS OF ST. PHILOMENA

Cemeteries are not as bleak as you might first think. If you've ever leisurely walked through one, taking the time to look closely at those apparently nondescript tombstones, there are names and dates on them, a history marking the life and death of countless individuals. Did you ever stop to think that each stone sequesters a story, an unbroken chain of events which describes in minute detail the unique character of a person? If those tombstones could speak, if a gravesite could contact the world, it might offer more lasting memory, marked for eternal time and never to be forgotten, about the individual whose brief sojourn is in their keeping.

No life, no matter its apparent insignificance, is without worth, a contribution to the whole of things. The individual is enhanced by the group and takes meaning from the forward movement and accomplishment of every member of the community. Whoever lives and dies leaves something of meaning, a unique offering to those who will come after, adding to what has been and making way for what is yet to come.

When I died, I was not buried in a cemetery. My resting place isn't graced by sprawling green lawns and quiet, remote landscape. There is no hushed peace, broken only by birdsong and the distant hum of city life. I have gone back too quickly into the grist of the world. You cannot bury bricks and mortar, stained glass and varnished pews, lay them quietly beneath the fallow earth. I have no tombstone to mark my passage, to offer testimony that I lived, breathed and generated life in the hearts of a multitude who faithfully counted me as "home."

I am a church. My tombstone, if I had one, would be situated

1

on a vacant lot at East Fourteenth Avenue and Detroit Street in Denver, where I used to live. Such shallow information might at first seem unimpressive, a passing fact whose clamor for recognition hardly deserves a second thought. Briefest reflection, however, would reveal that the record of my existence and history can be found in the life and spirit of every person who walked through my doors and sat down to imbibe the purpose of my tenure on this time-bound earth. It was my happy charge to bring what is eternal and immutable into the temporary and capricious lives of my family, the congregation, the members who, in their turn, nurtured and cared for me in countless ways. I stood as absolute, an irrefrangible contact with the very presence and touch of God, the divine, amidst so much which is too human, shot through with imprecision and flaw.

My stone, if I had one, would contain the simplest of epitaphs: "St. Philomena, a Church of Happy Memory, 1911 to 1984. Here is a Church whose memory still resides in the hearts of many. There is no death, only life ever breathing in those who shared the breath of this humble place." As you know, such meager phrases can serve only as a beginning. It is the story behind the stone, deeper than mere words, which must be counted and remarked. It is my story which I hope to tell in some halting measure because it deserves its place in history. It seems necessary to me because it is a story of people, the flesh and bone of my being, the pulsing of the tens of thousands who found respite and rejuvenation within my walls. Their identity has become mine, a melange of connections better identified as many persons who make up one, who gave me being and essence.

It seems possible to my imperfect thinking that the simplest reason for not having a stone or formal burial and ritual prayers, is that I have not died. I am still there, living on those corner lots, occupying the hearts and spirits of those who remember me. I will ever be there, if not in stone, then cast in the more granite guise of immortality of soul, the church on the Corner, St. Philomena's, of happy memory, past and present, leaning eagerly into the future and always remembering, with something to tell which bears hearing and reflection.

My name is St. Philomena. I must hasten to declare that I am not a saint in the essential sense of the word. How can a church — walls and towers, cornices and faded linoleum floors — contain anything of the virtue and sanctity ordinarily attributed to those we call saints? There is a certain holiness, however, about my very being, something akin to identity through long association. If my name has significance, if I possess a specific odor of goodness, it is because of the people who were housed here, offered shelter away from their busy lives, who found in me something of their better selves.

I was named after a martyr, a woman with whose memory and person I have become very comfortable over more than seventy years. St. Philomena, the holy woman in question, lived in or near Rome many centuries ago. Little more is known of her than that she lay for years under her own stone which read simply: "Sancta Filumena, Martyris." That simple phrase offered evidence to those who found her unidentified body that she was a person of prominence and notoriety. I suppose they found her while moving bodies from one cemetery to another, perhaps to what was thought to be holier ground, easier resting place for saints.

It is entirely conceivable that the early Christian community was happy to find another saint, and swiftly added her name to the ranks of those already deemed worthy of such honors. If one stumbles over this reasoning, consider: in those times there were not enough saints to go 'round, thus obviously there were fewer stipulations for canonization than in these days of ritual and formality. Today it is not easy to become a saint. It takes much more than a nondescript marker. Let it be that life was simpler then and that through such neglect I received my name, for which I am happy and grateful.

One is not a saint for a day, lasting awhile, then receding back into the folds of time, lost and forgotten. Sainthood goes on and validates itself in what comes after. I am confident that my own sanctity (or is it that of St. Philomena?), perhaps better stated "our sanctity," is confirmed by the people who came here to this church which has become my person. My suspicion is that most of those who have "come in" over the years have been every bit as good as the saints on official rosters. It is my further presumption that those saints "up there" wouldn't mind saying it, least of all St. Philomena. Even as I repeat it, I think I can feel something of her gentle spirit inside, down deep, the kindness of her sensitive acceptance that we are all saints, together constituting a holiness which transcends the virtue of the individual.

A surprising number of people are saints. I would like to tell you about some of them, but I couldn't do that were I compelled to stand by the letter of the law and maintain strict observance of what we have come imperiously to call "theology." Such a rigid approach centers emphasis on who can be canonized and who must remain in those well defined margins of runners-up. You see, most all of us are imperfect in at least some small way or another. It is my conjecture that St. Philomena was, too. It is ludicrous to assume that she was a model of perfection with no family tensions, no anger or dislocation over the miscues of neighbors, no bad days and no unbidden daily obstacles.

The kind of saints I got to meet, who came here over the years, were more like what you'd expect human beings to be. Most were good, some a bit foolish, but basically struggling to get something from life, to give a little and leave something of their spirit behind.

So you see, my life and times as a church were rather pleasant. With all that goes on, the pitch and hum of a thousand different events — weddings, funerals, births, deaths, beginnings and ends — I got to know the heighth and depth of every emotion, of laughter abruptly ending in weeping over the loss of a friend, a husband or wife. I was visited by a variety of people never found most places. Bishops came occasionally, an Apostolic Delegate here and there, Priors and Abbots, religious superiors, nuns and priests infinite in scope and kind. I will undoubtedly tell you stories you may not believe. I tried sometimes to close my old and blistered ears, but couldn't always, and have heard some confessions best left locked in my heart forever.

At first sight, it might seem that I was like any other church.

I was built around 1914 and looked like what you'd expect a church to be: blond brick, stained glass, and twin towers that originally rose above the homes in my neighborhood. But, with the age of high rise apartments, I lost something of my stature and looked pretty small under the arrogant gaze of many taller buildings.

Nor was there anything significantly distinguishing inside of me. The pews were just pews, scratched and worn dull by a thousand pious arms and posteriors, the weekly rhythm of standing, kneeling and gratefully sitting. I had an ample share of plaster statues (stern, over-painted saints) who took seriously their task of warning that heaven isn't easily won and beware of thoughts to the contrary.

If I take a deep breath and use my memory, I can still catch an odor of sanctity, smell something about churches and ceremonies you can't catch anywhere else. If I listen carefully, I can hear the shuffle and undertone of Sunday gatherings, a phrase or two of some old sermon still echoing around the rafters. Sometimes I get just a whiff of incense from a funeral or procession going around and out of the church. It's all there, inside, eternal and changeless.

If by now you are asking why I am going on like this, ranting a bit and perhaps waxing a bit sentimental, there is a justifiable, entirely reasonable answer. I've been demolished, you see, torn down to make way for progress. I share the plight of other churches, of old and noble homes, timeless buildings, marking the great events of city life. We're gone now, unremembered and forgotten. It seems a pity.

But you really can't destroy a building, take it away as though it never existed. Oh, you can raze the bricks and mortar, but you can't take away what is deeper, what transcends the mute materials that give life to what is inside. It is true the structure comes down, topples to the excruciating pain of the wrecking ball. But a building is more than mindless stone and wood. It is people inside, the long line of pulsing human beings who visited there, gave it life, engendered breath and spirit, made it laugh and weep for the capricious joys and sorrows inextricably entwined into the fabric of its mystery.

Though you may not see me again the way I used to be, standing tall and majestic, I am there all the same. My life is in my memory, enough to last forever. It is good and gives consolation, peace with something to cry or laugh over on lonely nights when I miss the presence of my former self.

I know I am still here. I could never be convinced otherwise. It seems entirely important to me not to let you forget, either. You owe me more than careless storage to the back of your mind until I fade into oblivion. You took too much from me to let me disappear into the mists of time.

I deserve better, a church of quiet retreat where people found something missing in the rest of life. I have marked your growth and progress through time. You can't simply treat me as though I had never been.

If you listen (strain just a little) you can hear a bell softly toll to signal the beginning of the end of some phase of life at St. Philomena's. I was a peaceful place. God was here. We believed it, and we kept telling others who came. That was enough to make it real.

I stood bravely here more than seventy years, a long time to be anywhere, to be watching and reeling to the buzz of life. I've watched horses clatter up the old streets around here and then disappear, giving way to the pop and chug of Model T and A Fords, the streetcar and the raucous motorcycle, the busy hum of life. And I've liked it. I creaked and sagged a little, lost some of my youthful gait, but I was around a long time and count my days a blessing.

Lately, I've suffered a little blurring about some of the things which happened long ago and I'm better about what is more recent. I can't get it all just right anymore. There has been too much, too many people, an incalculable quantity of goings-on. I can't remember some names I used to know as well as my own. I'm positive there's a story inside me and perhaps it will become clearer as I tell it.

It seems so important now to let my history out, to tell it and be finished. I'll never forget it all and I want you to remember. If there is no room for an old church like me, I ought at least to have the chance to say a few things. Isn't that reasonable?

Chapter Two

AND THEN GOD MADE PASTORS

The first words I remember are, "Dammit Phil, you did it!"
That might seem a little incongruous on the face of it, especially
coming from a priest, Michael Donovan, the first pastor and
the person to whom I owe my existence. You must understand,
he had been in the army and old soldiers have an excuse, I
suppose, for using strong language. "Dammit" was mild, I think,
for him.

The story has it that Michael had been hoping to build a
church. There was then, as there is now, a maze of red tape
to be cut for such a project. Not least among the hurdles is
getting the money, or part of it, before one can begin. The day
came when Michael finally received permission, money, or both
after he had been praying to St. Philomena, a favorite of his
but a little-known saint. Perhaps pastors like to think they have
a direct route with prayers of petition. It is a conviction from
which I have never wanted to dissuade them. Michael was sure
St. Philomena had done it all. He came home in a rush of
enthusiasm that day, shouting what could hardly be termed an
invective, "Dammit, Phil, you did it!"

It was 1911, a vintage year. It was the year Irving Berlin gave
us "Alexander's Ragtime Band," ushering in a new era of
American Jazz. Rome's Victor Emmanuel Monument was
completed after twenty-eight years of construction. Taliesin East,
a feat of unparalleled architecture, was completed by Frank Lloyd
Wright. New York City's $9 million Public Library main branch
was presented by architect Thomas Hastings. New York's Ellis
Island had a record one-day influx of 11,745 immigrants on April
17, 1911. St. Philomena's Church, twin towers, vaulted ceiling,

choir loft, spacious sanctuary and complete linoleum floor, was built in 1911, taking its place among all those other august and gracious happenings.

Dramatic beginnings are always more so in retrospect. I don't suppose Columbus thought it such a big affair when he set out from Genoa, or Barcelona. It might have seemed another routine trip to him. The beginning of my life was likely similar to many other beginnings. There is a moment when the seed is planted and given the potential of fruition. I wouldn't want to be dramatic, even now, except that history was in the making and wouldn't stop until we had seen more changes than we could ever have anticipated. Any day is the brink of realities to come. Perhaps we treat life too casually and attain less from it than had we given it a little more drama from the start.

Of course, we are fond of thinking life has more to offer because of our presence in the world. It cannot be different with a church. Forgive me. I sometimes fantasize that it all could not have happened without me. Is it presumptious to say that more has happened in the past seventy-five years in religion and the spirit of people than in the first two thousand? Perhaps such rash assertions should be tempered with greater humility. But consider the history of the last century: population explosions, rising religious consciousness, two world wars and many minor (if such a term is applicable to war of any sort) conflagrations, the rush of technology, religious renewals, revivals, meetings of the minds, various kinds of estrangements and schisms. To say it couldn't have happened without me is simply to admit my small but important part in it. In almost seventy-three years, I have experienced a veritable myriad of currents and directions which often took strength and movement in the many who came to visit within my walls. I have creaked and moaned with the weight of it all, going through cold winters and hot summers, the best and worst of times. I stood, until recently, and made my contribution.

In 1911 the heave and sway of building began. It was my birth. As with everyone, I have only a hazy recollection of those beginning years. I must rely heavily on others who remember the story better. I have the distinct impression that I was built with loving hands, tender care, to endure. That I lasted well is amply attested by those who were my family, who said that I was as good on the day they tore me down as I was the day they opened my doors.

I was dedicated in 1912. This meant, simply, that I was approved, deemed fit for my own purpose and could thenceforth be called a "Church," a name whose impact has always been held in reverence and esteem in spite of blatant abuses by some few. It was surely a day of celebration. A host of people gathered there — many priests, even a bishop who pronounced me fit and said any number of prayers for my longevity and effectiveness. The bishop put in the last brick and advised the faithful to see in me their home, a friend, a place of welcome and refuge. If I am fabricating some of that, not remembering it all accurately, it is because I have a notion of how it should have been. I'd like to add in my own behalf that the bishop might have said churches are eternal, indestructible, built to last forever. I know surely that here I am leaning toward wishful thinking. I know surely, also, that you will understand my motivation.

It is my romantic reflection that I began very effectively, was everything a church building should be. People came immediately and loved my appearance. They talked about how comforting it was to have their own church and found something new in their identity with me. They came to sit gently in my pews, ran their hands affectionately along the backs of the seats with a sigh of satisfaction. There is an indescribable solace that arises from acceptability. I had achieved something of status and honor. What more could one ask?

From the beginning I was well used, made to feel the center of activity. We had two masses on Sunday, devotions, prayers, novenas, benedictions, missions, retreats and whatever else is pertinent to a beginning, growing church. I was a busy place, with much coming and going, never locked in those days, my doors always open and offering welcome.

Eventually I was blessed with an organ, neatly placed in my choir loft. The music was an added fortune and we all relished it, the people and I. Sometimes late at night, when the world was asleep, the organ and I talked about how our life was going. The organ offered no real complaints, only wheezed occasionally over some musician's heavy foot or the miscalculation of a sharp for a flat, bringing some pain to its members and causing it to ache a little on nights when the cold weather set in.

Michael was a good pastor, relished what he did, respected and loved the people. After a time he was given an assistant, the first of what seems an infinite number.

Johnny was a small, humble man who wrung his fingers and hands endlessly, as though apologizing for his intrusive presence in anyone's life. He struck me as always nervous and a little afraid, which prompted Michael to even more bluster and oratory.

I remember clearly the day Michael took him around, showed him my interior, where everything could be found. At that moment, had I not known before, I came to realize that Michael was a good friend. He began their tour by loudly shouting instructions to Johnny, "Remember," he said officiously, "this is a church. So take care of it, dammit." (I think it was his favorite word, or perhaps he was using it often in lieu of others even less desirable. It made me wince some, but I knew he was only wanting to emphasize.)

He continued: "I have a great devotion to the Blessed Sacrament, dammit, so keep this place clean, ship-shape. Understand?" I knew that Johnny did, because he wrung his hands vigorously and said "yes" three or four times, very quickly.

Those were good years. Michael stayed until 1922. We went through the first World War and he had to return to the army for a while, but we won the war and thought winning was everything. Michael was sure that wars were over, finished once and forever.

Michael came back safe, hearty and none the worse for it all. He had changed little: lots of dammits and a liberal sprinkling of other loud expletives. He was by now an old friend and our separation enkindled an even closer spirit. In those early days after the war he came over at odd times and just walked around, examined my structure and wear, reassuring himself that I was enduring well and offering no extraordinary worry.

It is a phenomenon of the life of any church that pastors do not last forever. Here, as perhaps everywhere, life suffers those interruptions which change existing conditions, hopefully for good, but never guaranteed. Simply put, a day came when Michael left for another church, another assignment of service to other people. It is that way with pastors and brings a mixture of blessings. For those who are chafing under the direction of an abrasive shepherd, change brings new hope and a spark of freshness. For those who love their pastor, there is disappointment and apprehension about who is to come.

When it was rumored that Michael was to leave, a vague tension took hold of the people and me. Conditions of that nature are always at least a bit traumatic. We gave ourselves over to copious anxiety. Some more pious individuals came to whisper a prayer that the coming pastor wouldn't be too hard on them, not say whatever it was which made people leave the church in a huff and shake the dust of the parish off their feet. Some prayed he wouldn't talk too much about money and be one of those priests who said that weekly contributions were the most important element in any parish and that tithing was the only sure way to heaven. Others prayed that we would not have to endure the resumption of sermons on sin and how most of us were destined for hell with no hope of salvation except through the extraordinary grace of a merciful God, who gave favors discriminately and not at all by sheer generosity. We were a fretting and worrisome community.

We could have saved our energy. When the new pastor came, ending those days of apprehension, we couldn't afford the time to remember our anxious anticipation. There was so much immediate and consuming activity that most people were caught up in something which wasn't to end for over forty years.

Willie came in 1922 and stayed until he died. Even with his death, I couldn't be sure that he was finished here. What happened is a complete history in itself and could fill at least a book.

To say that Willie was different is an egregious understatement and does him a disservice. To say he was unique is weak. There was simply never anyone comparable to Willie. To whom or what could I liken him? Certainly not to other priests or other pastors in neighboring parishes. They claimed there was no mold for Willie. They said that with Willie, God attempted something new. I think it is absolutely true.

How does one begin? What could I say to you about Willie, to do justice to what he was, who he was? There is too much of it, inside, a part of my life, inextricably interwoven there. It is impossible to tell the story of Willie without telling my own. Even as I offer this, I am aware that I fall short of what I want to say. Willie wouldn't have a story, nor would I, except for the people, the chapters you might say, of his life. Willie was to become so much a part of the people, so intimately immersed in their lives that, somehow, there was no real distinction between him and them. Oh, he retained his unusual self, never gave up his own identity, but his life wound around the people so closely that they took him to be an essential part of their lives.

Willie was born at the perfect time to be the person he was. I mean to be a pastor, shepherd a flock, lead the people of a parish, offer an abundance of guidance and hurried wisdom to the assistant priests who lived here. It certainly couldn't happen now. In those earlier days religion was far more prominent in the lives of the great majority of people. God was a household word. One's sojourn through life was tightly knit with religious sentiment and sprang out of deep faith. Because such conviction abounded, religion was generously mixed into the traditions of God's close presence, exaggerated authority, absolute beliefs, sure and consistent answers, and the solid notion that believers were the favored group, looking to salvation and release from the cares of the world. We had a lot to learn but were not in the mood for it in those years. We were sure of ourselves and knew for sure where we were going.

Willie fit into that scheme of things perfectly. How could I describe him? I cannot, except to say that he was a bittersweet mixture of everything very human and flawed, yet deeply gifted, willing but falling short of simplest ideals, courageous and afraid, strong yet weak, close but vaguely distant. He was like most people, yet beyond most. In my imperfect judgment, he had more to carry than others, more weight of some kind. There was some sort of unease in him, a sense of intensity and compulsion over what he couldn't somehow discern. There must have been something in his background, trailing perhaps to his youth, which made him the way he was. He was pleasing but never sure he had pleased; generous, but uncertain what his motives were; personal and warm, yet afraid to accept the warmth and regard of others. He was not a simple person. It is precisely because of this that most of us loved him. Whatever faults he had were generously compensated for by his intentions and goodwill. Obviously he was unforgettable and the source of countless stories. I can recount only a fraction of them.

With this medley of unpredictable ingredients, there were times I wanted to speak to him, to hint that he could do some things better. I never had the courage. He was responsible for me, had my fate in his hands. Above all, he was good — to everyone. What more can I say except that he took care of me. In his over forty years he absolutely would never let anything deteriorate. I was painted, decorated, my windows leaded and refurbished, my floors waxed and polished regularly. He let nothing go. Some, especially some assistants, used to make light of his efforts and say (among themselves) that he seemed to think administration was the major task of the pastor and, as long as he was doing something, spending a little of the people's money, had a project in progress, he was proving his worth. One overly witty resident sardonically remarked that my pews were varnished so often they would stand alone if there were some miraculous way to take the wood out from under the varnish. From long years of practice, I have become accustomed to humor of that sort from assistants.

Willie wasn't easy on assistants. He expected much from them, demanded more than the usual pastor. Some thought he was a bit unfair, but Willie never thought of himself as mean or unjust. He came from a background which maintained that, when you are pastor, you are the highest authority in the parish in every sense of the word. No one could really dislike him or put him out of the realm of contact. He wouldn't let that happen. He was there, kept coming back, no matter how often. If there was any difficulty, it was caused by the fact that one never knew exactly what Willie was going to do from day to day. He changed, the way we all do, but more radically, more precipitously. It kept us all just a little off balance, kept us from completely relaxing.

For all that and more, for all his apparent faults, it was easier to remember the good in him. There was always enough to help us accept his faults. I think the most remarkable of his many gifts was his open and unending generosity. When he died, I don't think he had more than a few dollars, even though much money had passed through his hands during his lifetime. His room was bare and ascetic, no lavish fixtures, nothing extra of any kind. Sometimes he spent prodigally, but never on himself. People said he didn't know the value of money. But he was generous. If anyone needed anything, he gave it without question if he had it. He saw these occasions of need as opportunities, something of a reflection of the gospel.

Here's but one example, Mamie, a long-standing parishioner, worked hard, saved her money and retired in her old age. When she died, she left all she had to Willie. Her entire substance came to a little over fourteen thousand dollars. When that happened, many years ago, such a sum was considerably more impressive than it would be today.

Mamie's bequest offered Willie a singular, consoling message: she thought he was a true pastor, interested and sensitive and that what he did was edifying to her, added something to her life she had never received anywhere else. Mamie never married. She wasn't, by far, the most attractive woman on the block nor the most popular person in the parish. We expect the wealthy to bequeath their riches to worthy and holy causes. It is an opportunity to pay their debt. We reason that since God was good to them they, in turn, incur what is akin to an obligation to be generous.

Mamie wasn't rich. She wasn't famous or prominent. She worked daily, undoubtedly wearily (for the telephone company, I think). Had you seen her on the streetcar, in church or walking down the street, you might have just passed her by and never given her another thought. She fit neatly into crowds, merely another person, a common face, nothing distinguishing about her appearance or dress.

Willie gave Mamie something no one else did, or even wanted to. He made her feel fine about herself, told her she was a virtuous woman, a good Christian, had done a remarkable job at life — had done her part. Some people accused Willie of overstating the truth at times, of offering lavish praise where a little more objectivity would have been better. I used to think that he and I weren't seeing the same person when he'd declare how beautiful someone was, or how intelligent. I came to understand, in time, this was Willie's way of making people feel confident in themselves, to begin to perceive that they weren't ordinary after all.

He did that for Mamie, and scores of others — the little people, as we have come to call them, living alone, the old and forgotten, the widow, those who have no one to offer assistance, those who are hardly ever invited to Sunday dinner. They were Willie's kind of folks, the sort who are easily passed by and forgotten.

No wonder Mamie and others left him their money. Now if Willie had deposited it all safely in a bank, or taken a periodic trip to Europe with it, bought an imposing car every year, we might have criticized him and accused him of ulterior motives. But he didn't. He gave it away so quickly we hardly knew he had it.

So when Willie received the fourteen thousand dollars, he immediately began to give it away, here and there, five hundred or a thousand at a time. He made a donation to the missions and a sizable contribution to the Pope, perhaps for pragmatic reasons.

When Willie had about four thousand dollars left, a couple

came to the door of the rectory one day to say goodbye and thank Willie for the time they had spent in his parish. They were giving up their house because they couldn't keep up the payments, were several behind. They were returning to New Mexico and protested that they probably shouldn't have moved to Denver because it was too expensive. Willie asked how much they owed on their house. Three payments, they replied. He said, "No, not how many payments, but how much on the entire house?" They said it was a sizeable amount some eight or nine thousand dollars. He then rocked them into disbelief and shock by telling them he was going to give them four thousand dollars and could they renegotiate the loan to smaller payments? He said, simply, he hoped they would remain in the parish because he liked them and their seven children and wanted them in the school.

What could they do, except protest weakly, cry some and accept the money? What could Willie do, except say a few gruff words, pretend that it was all insignificant and dramatically terminate the meeting because he had "some things to do" — go the the hospital and see Mary, and then Edward, because they were sick and he wanted to see how they were.

In the face of that sort of generosity, it is difficult to speak about Willie's faults. Somehow, it seems a little disloyal, unfaithful to something in him which was good and memorable. He was human, admittedly, and had his share of shortcomings. He had a kind of fever inside, something which told him he wasn't quite adequate, that he had to prove himself. So he tried, perhaps too hard, to please and indulge. He was ordinarily so responsive to the parish, to the people in his life, it might be that he felt he had a tantrum or two occasionally coming to him, a justified outburst for all that he had done.

At these times he came over to me to speak of it, to talk about how he wanted to renew his resolutions to maintain a calmer exterior. It is arrogant to dramatize these moments, but I felt a part of what was happening. I tried in my own way to be warm and receptive, as much as a church can. I wanted just to be there, to let God do the talking and listening. Willie would sometimes cry a little, especially when he got older and could be more honest about his confusions. He just couldn't get over the fact that he was so human. When these sessions would evolve in my presence, I had the feeling that we sometimes demand too much of one another and, perhaps more lamentable, we demand too much of ourselves.

The last privelege given to churches like me is the opportunity of philosophizing. No one has ever asked me to offer my analysis of a complex situation. Far better on my part simply to sit quietly and appear pious, which I can certainly do. But if anyone is interested, I have this to say: Perhaps if persons like Willie — priests, ministers and such, maybe anyone at all — had a chance to be a little more human, to accept themselves for what they are, to let their seamier side show some, they might be better for it. That is what I think. I'm not an expert, but I was seventy-two before they tore me down. That should count for something.

Well, if you put it all together in one place, I mean Willie's life and all that surrounded it, you would have to say that the good so out shone the bad that it hardly cast a shadow. I like to remember it all: earliest mornings, someone coming to open up for six o'clock mass, lighting the candles and making small sounds so as not to disturb the lingering night. I remember the people coming in, slowly, quietly, the start of a new day. They came in little knots and groups, families, single people. Older parishioners came early, to say their special prayers and just be quiet. They were followed by mothers and fathers with their children, then the young, just in time or a little late for mass.

Those days always started fresh and hopeful. I came to love it, grew up with it and never tired of its consistency and dependability. It was the time when Willie and all the rest — assistants, workers, parishioners — were at their very best.

It was a good life I had. I would do it all again, without hesitation or condition. There was something about it all I can't describe, but I'll try.

One thing is certain. It was sacred, holy somehow. I don't mean pious, sanctimonious, over-religious. It was holy in the best sense of the word. I used to say that if God could ever be found it was there, in those people, in what they brought and what they took with them when they left.

Chapter Three

SOME PERHAPS UNPONDERED NOTIONS

There is really no such reality as a church. There is, of course, a roof and walls, foundation and specific dimensions. But for all that, a church is something which finds its existence in the people who come there. Just by mentioning the nàme St. Philomena's, for example, a whole set of images is conjured: the people, the priests and staff, even the mood that the church presents.

A church is really a personality, more than an impassive structure of sterile building materials. Sometimes I've heard people say, "That's a good church," or "I know a church you'll like to attend." What they mean, of course, is that the people there are good, likeable and easy to get to know, that the Sunday mass and other services are pleasant to attend, that the people who work there are, most times, reasonable and friendly.

I've always thought that pastors should take note of these truths, take them to heart and understand that they have more to do with what a church is than anyone. A church simply doesn't exist on its own, apart from the people who go there, the pastor who has the care of the congregation, the assistants and staff who contribute day to day.

In my case, I was blessed, I think, with a continuing line of interested and sensitive people. It is a fortune sometimes not immediately apparent in churches. I've heard about some which don't enjoy a reputation for feeling and understanding. This certainly wasn't the case with me. The mere mention of "St. Philomena's" made most respond positively, with some supportive comment. If I were to assess the reasons for my good reputation, it would be based in part on what Willie and the rest of the people who worked here did.

Being a pastor is not a simple duty. I've never heard that Jesus gave specific instructions on what that role entails. There is nothing in the scriptures about budgets, building and maintenance, schools and education. Some mention is made of personal qualities, like being guileless as doves and wise as serpents. There are exhortations to be forgiving, loving and generous. There is a command to be prayerful, to offer peace and harmony rather than hatred and rejection. There are even warnings about being misunderstood and persecuted. But there is no mention of second collections, building commissions, the visit of the bishop, letters from the pope or the search for a suitable school principal. Being a good pastor or assistant or member of the staff is a learning process, not subject to a simple formula.

For all that I can say of Willie, among the most important is that he was a sensitive and good man. I have already described him in terms of his generosity and sensitive response to people in need. The stories about Mamie and those parishioners who couldn't make their house payments could be repeated many times, only changing the persons and circumstances. How can I describe Willie except to say, as I have already, that he had a generous heart and thought of others before himself. He had the great, perhaps rare, human characteristic of liking people and wanting to serve them. He was pleased to be with them. There were times when he hurt some individuals by being too brusque or heavy-handed. He certainly didn't mean to. He was over-sensitive and worried too much. Sometimes he lost sleep fretting over some remark he'd made in a rush of enthusiasm or bluster. Most of the people knew him well enough to overlook those inconsistencies and were amply compensated by what he did for them. We all understood that in forty years in one place he was bound to make some mistakes. That kind of frailty came with his occupation.

In the days when Willie started, being a pastor had its own kind of thinking and disposition. It meant a person of authority and highest respect from the people. Faith and the practiced response of parishioners was one of submission and deference. A pastor assumed an unusual amount of dignity and power. His word had sacred and, in many cases, irreversible impact. His word was law and no one argued much with him in those earlier years. Parishioners dared not say anything in opposition to him.

You might think that it was difficult for most pastors not to be affected by this traditional thinking about their importance. It is not easy to live with the constant insistence that one is better than others, has assumed a higher station than the average person. There is a danger there, having to do with the subtle persuasion that what people say and believe is actually true. One tends, in that position, to forget his or her own weaknesses, those human qualities which equalize and remind us that we share what is imperfect with the rest of humankind.

If this was true of Willie, it is understandable. Somehow he had the notion, I think, that what he was, his own sense of dignity, his role, redounded to the people, made them better, uplifted them and gave them a sense of their own identity with the Church and what was holy. Willie felt that he was important, no doubt about it. He loved to put on the robes signifying that he was a Monsignor, a title of honor and impact. He even had a little purple patch beneath his white collar to indicate that he held that title. I wouldn't want to imply that he was proud with all that word suggests. He simply thought that being a Monsignor was an important part of the Church which he loved and to which he devoted himself.

There are two classes of Monsignor. I didn't realize that until one evening when an incident took place which illustrates rather well that Willie was, after all, a human being. It was a First Friday, a special day among Catholics for devotion and mass during the week. Willie said the evening mass and went to the rectory for supper. It was summertime, windows open, offering easy hearing of whatever was happening in the rectory. I knew when Willie left after mass that he was in something of an agitated state. It was a trait of his to become sort of noisy, moving furniture and odd objects around, aimlessly, ventilating accumulated energy.

Willie had different ways of entering the house, giving his own signal about what was uppermost in his mind. Experience immediately indicated what state he was in. On this occasion he entered hurriedly, let the door slam ominously, and paused at the door of the kitchen. Two assistants were in the dining room eating halibut, Friday's offering for penance and good works. As I remember, no words were actually spoken, but mutual and comprehensive communication passed between them. They looked at each other in understanding that this night might be longer than usual.

As this silent interchange passed between them, they could hear Willie speaking oratorically to Stella, the housekeeper. He reminded her about spending too much time with the flowers and the apple trees outside and that he'd asked her before to comply with his wishes, and was she prepared to respond?

When he entered the dining room with his quick flourish, eyes bright and face set in determination, the assistants knew certainly that the weather was not to be the topic of conversation that evening. To appropriate silence he began: "I am a Monsignor. Not simply a Papal Chamberlain (the first and obviously lesser type). I am a Domestic Prelate (the second and more dignified type). Do you know what I just did?" Silence. Looks of apprehension overtook the assistants' eyes. Forks were gently laid aside. A polite use of the napkin for etiquette, an unobtrusive clearing of the throat. Expectation. "I just put a mop away," Willie said. Then, silence for dramatic effect.

"I have two assistants . . . who could walk over that mop repeatedly, trip on it, and never put it away. I'm a Domestic Prelate. And I put it away."

There ensued a listing of deficiencies and shortcomings in the lives of those two parish priests, their apparent apathy and the dire need for improvement in their sensibilities and general acumen. Would they mind taking notice when work needed to be done, and please execute it? There followed allusions to earlier occasions when they had been lacking and needed to be reminded that certain responses were naturally expected of them. Examples of inefficiency were liberally offered amid intermittent expostulations over what the world was coming to.

In the short silence that settled when Willie had finished, one of the assistants, the braver of the two I suspect, said, almost inaudibly, "Why don't you get a janitor?" Willie, after his strident outburst, wasn't expecting anyone to comment and had to ask the assistant to repeat what he had just said. More clearly now, the assistant offered his bold comment a second time. "I said, why don't you get a janitor?"

Whatever hope anyone had of finishing the halibut vanished and everyone present, including Stella, who was listening intently behind the swinging door, knew that more was to come. The other assistant was thinking gratefully of his convert class to begin in just forty-five minutes and to last until after nine. He prayed silently that conditions of tranquility would prevail by that time. Perhaps matters would be settled and forgotten.

Sometimes, in winter especially, when my doors were closed and voices from the house were muffled, I had to wait for fuller details about what happened there. Explanations and clarification came when one or the other members of the household came over to pray, or just to sit and speak silently to God. On this particular night, however, I heard everything very clearly. I think some of the other buildings and people up the block did, too.

After the assistant's question there was a protracted silence, perhaps fifteen seconds, which seemed much longer. Willie, at these times, had a mannerism of contorting his mouth, as though he were grinding his teeth, but without the accompanying sound. It gave the impression that his patience was heavily taxed by having to deal with such mundane, inconsequential matters as the flippant remarks of an uncomprehending assistant.

One might construe that a remark about hiring a janitor was entirely reasonable, but circumstances of normal interchange didn't often exist between assistants and pastors. Unwritten law stipulated that the pastor was superior, at least in authority, and had the irrefrangible right of saying what he wanted without interruption. It was a remarkable system, readily tolerated by most priests because they waited patiently for that blessed day when they, in their own turn, would become pastors.

What happened when the assistant made that apparently innocent suggestion caused such consternation that what Willie said and what the assistant said in return are best left to the sands of time. In most contexts, it would not have been considered that shocking. It was like any family quarrel, intense, with unintended hurt and expletives. Willie had the upper hand and he knew it. He finally ordered the assistant, about fifty years old, to go to his room. He went obediently, where he stayed and whistled off-key, a talent with which he was blessed and which was especially apparent when he was nervous. Sometimes he sang a sort of tune which sounded like "heydi heydi ho," dropping the "ho" to a lower register, over and over again.

He stayed in his room whistling and singing for about a half-hour. Finally, Willie went up to his room, perhaps because the whistling and inconsequential tune served notice that he was quarantined until further notice. There was, of course, the added note that the storm had passed and Willie wanted to settle and forget. Knowing him as I did, I realized that he was beginning to feel that remorse which crept stealthily into his conscience after such tempests.

I could not exactly determine what they said to each other because the assistant's room was on the far side of the house. I do know that somehow, equanimity was restored and a sense of peace came over their lives again. The other assistant went to his class that evening, among other issues, teaching the distinction between Papal Chamberlains and Domestic Prelates. The ever-roaming cats in the alley ate halibut that night and by eleven or so the scene was dark and quiet. The last sounds I heard in the darkness of late night were a just-off-key rendition of "heydi heydi ho." At midnight, all was still and I had the impression everyone over there was asleep, except maybe Willie, who had a tendency to brood and wonder what life was really about.

There is a certain hierarchy interwoven into any church and parish structure. The pastor, of course, occupies the highest level of responsibility and dignity. You might expect that immediately under him are the assistants, but that simply isn't true, at least not in those earlier days. An assistant had to be in residence only a short time to discern that not only was he not next in line to the pastor, but far down the ladder of impact.

In most cases, and certainly in ours, the person who stood imperiously close to the top of things was the housekeeper. Such a design was not nearly so ludicrous as one might think. In most cases she enjoyed the longest tenure of anyone in the house, except perhaps for the pastor himself. One word which might adequately describe her stalwart fidelity is "endurance." She somehow was among the most adjustable of all people, learning to integrate and accept the idiosyncrasies of any and all priests who came to live within the shadow of her realm. No wonder she assumed an importance exceeding that of the assistants. They would come and go, but she conceivably could remain forever, or at least a reasonable facsimile of what forever might be.

In my time there was a number of housekeepers, taking their place for what they assumed would be a permanent position. For one reason or another, though, they lasted for shorter periods than hoped. That, I have come to assume, was because there is a certain substance or timber with which housekeepers are born that belongs to only a chosen few. Stella, who reigned here (if that is an appropriate word) for over forty years, was the only bonafide housekeeper I ever knew. I had the impression that she was born a housekeeper and could not imagine a time when she was a child or had ever done anything other than her chosen profession.

Stella. It means "star" in Latin, and fit her personality rather neatly. Anyone who would remain and enjoy the challenge so long should certainly be recognized as a star of some sort. The less respectful assistants used to call her "Stella the Bella Puella," translated "Stella, the Beautiful Girl," which she certainly was not, outside anyway. Certainly she had a beautiful soul, but she was not beautiful in the passing, shallow sense in which we over-use that word. She was strong; strong-minded and strong-willed. She had a way of remaining fixed in her opinions and thoughts. The priest here, even Willie most times, offered her fitting deference and latitude. To criticize the way she cooked and cared for the house was a challenge most did not accept.

Stella was from an old German Iowa family, where duty and religion came first. If I had to use one word, only one, to describe her, it would be "frugal." Frugality was as much a part of her innate makeup as her hands or her heart. She saved everything, from a piece of string to the last five peas in a bowl after supper. She had boxes of assorted items stored in nooks and corners around the house. It sometimes became the bane of Willie's existence. He knew, though, that if he wanted any odd and sometimes scarce object from the smallest safety pin to an off-sized box for wrapping, if Stella didn't have it, they just didn't make it any more.

A certain paradox, inscrutable and mysterious, existed in Stella's life. Though she was a housekeeper of long standing and drew her identity heavily from that state and vocation, working tirelessly at the most demanding labors, she hated to cook. Incomprehensible as that might seem, there was an obvious explanation. She'd cooked for so long, put so many meals together and for so many contrasting appetites, some not so delicate and others unreasonably fastidious, she just grew weary of it all. It turned out, in later life, she had too many other important projects to pursue. She loved being outside. She spent every available moment puttering in the dirt and flowers around the rectory, trimming the apple tree and sneaking a tomato plant here and there into the patches of flowers. Once she had a fierce quarrel with Willie over an apple tree she planted without his permission. Over a period of three days it was taken out and replanted four times. But Stella won and the tree grew up to offer an abundance of apples, which she harvested and peeled and preserved and put into pies and jelly and apple butter for weeks, working every day flush up to supper, when she would stop for a bit to prepare something simple and unpretentious like hamburger patties or breaded fish. Immediately afterward, she'd return to the harvest. She never really left the Iowa farm. She loved the smell of the soil on her hands. It gave her a sense of her origin and made her feel she was at home.

If the first word to describe Stella is "frugal," the second is that she was "good," with a goodness hewn from a rock-like solidarity of character and conviction. Who knows why she wanted to be a housekeeper? Willie used to say, not entirely humorously, that she could have managed a corporation or been a president of some kind. Her devoted labor always seemed to me to be a thankless task. The priests who lived here treated her well enough, but priests are not among the most normal people in the world. Stella knew that and in reality sustained sore difficulty in loving them all. She tried. And she stayed on. I think she had this idea that by being a housekeeper she was accomplishing what was holy, requiring dedication. She must have thought that by doing her work and tolerating whatever that required, she was actually doing the work of God, something like being a part of the priesthood and ministry itself. Such reasoning wasn't a totally unrealistic way of viewing the situation. In the final summation of it all, the priests I knew who were effective and accomplished commendable objectives received generous support from people like Stella and the other women who worked in the house.

When Stella retired, it really wasn't retirement; she just stopped making those quick meals and had more time for the apple tree. She moved across the street, becoming a kind of housekeeper emeritus, if there is such a thing. We had other housekeepers, but they only lasted for a while and suddenly developed pressing reasons for leaving — to take care of a sick brother-in-law, go back to college (at sixty-six!) or an unexpected attack of arthritis.

People came and went over there in the house. My merging and sometimes indistinct recollection of things is that new faces appeared and old ones faded from the scene. Any number of assistants came in and out of focus. A visitor might appear for a day or two, perhaps for a week, having some objective in mind like a retreat or mission, preaching and leaving quickly. Among all those names and faces some remained as the world moved on. They became so much a part of life here that I couldn't conceive that we would be the same without their presence.

Alice was the secretary and bookkeeper who came daily after

lunch and stayed until evening. She worked methodically upstairs and offered a cheerful addition to what sometimes appeared a somber atmosphere. Amid all that bustle and serious activity of ministry, her high pitched, careless laugh was a welcome sound and lent credence to the conviction that human qualities were sorely needed in so much work and application.

How Alice came to be here, I can't remember. I only know that she appeared shortly after Willie arrived and was here as long as he was.

Ruth came evenings, shortly after Alice left, to answer the phone and do accounting. She was a small, soft-spoken woman whose great pleasure in life consisted in the joy of conversation with Willie and a few close friends. She was scrupulously devoted to her work and saw her place there as important, essential to the workings of what happened daily.

The women who worked here loved Willie. They depended on him to support them and ease their own misgivings about their worth to others. I had the impression they suffered from doubts about their role in life, tended to be anxious and sometimes depressed. Willie never tired of their demands, but sometimes grew irascible with their presumption that he would always solve their dilemmas. But he constantly offered them friendship and support.

Love is a difficult word to define and a definition sometimes has the wrong connotation of what it essentially is. It has so many facets it surely cannot be universally conceived or limited. I think the women in Willie's life loved him, in perhaps the most elevated sense possible. They saw in him something of what was holy, close to God, and in spite of his shortcomings, the wrinkles in his character, they accepted him without question or doubt.

As I cast backward, thinking again of all those years and experiences, I am flooded with the conviction that many people came into Willie's life who contributed much to him. We have the notion that priests give unhesitatingly, generously to others. And they do. There is a certain and sometimes more subtle reciprocity, however, which comes into clear focus in such matters of service and care. What priests and those in ministry give freely away, they receive, most times in far greater abundance, in return. I am sure that happened to Willie, and he was the first to admit it. He used to tell a story about an old Monsignor he knew who insisted that when he got down to almost no personal money, he would give it away with the confident anticipation that he would receive twice that in return through some unforeseen circumstance. The reason Willie told the story, it seems to me, is that he believed the same things happened to him, not necessarily in terms of money but in more important realities such as support and affirmation. I can vouch that it was so, having witnessed it often in what persons like Alice and Ruth and Stella gave to him.

Many other workers around these parts offered something of their personal qualities, gardeners, custodians, cleaning personnel, Sisters and other teachers, a host of people who constituted a family. They were a part of everything that took place here, the result of all of it being a mix of goodness which far outshone anything deficient.

I felt a part of it, even though I am an inanimate church building. The spirit here permeated even the most lifeless of things. What took place here gives me dynamism and spirit still. And it is very good.

Chapter Four

THE PECULIAR LIFE OF AN ASSISTANT

Times come and go. What was isn't any more, and what is now is only for a time. Nothing is permanent and perhaps the greatest peril in life is depending on the assumption that all things are stable and immutable.

Walking into a church these days, trying to catch the flavor of what is happening there, one finds it all quite different from what it was twenty-five years ago. Indeed, the meaning may still be there. What is essential remains. But the circumstances and character of things have undergone many transformations to make them more understandable and clearer.

In most parishes, life is a little easier, less formal and rigid than in times past. Maybe that comes from a deeper grasp of the significance of some traditions and rules that we simply accepted without question in former settings. In the Catholic Church, and I'm sure the same is true for other churches, people tolerated any rule or custom without doubt or resentment of any kind. They just presumed that everything was well established and reasonable, even if they didn't understand it.

Take as an example the Maniple. It was an integral part of the clothing which priests wore for Mass in earlier days. It was a garment draped over the left arm, completing the array of vestments for the sacred ceremony: amice, alb, cincture, stole, MANIPLE, chasuble.

What did the maniple signify? Not even the best informed Catholics could easily answer such a question. The maniple is nothing more than a carry-over from earlier days when people draped handkerchiefs over their arms as pockets weren't in vogue and they had to carry them someplace. How it came to be a vestment for sacred ceremonies, no one knows for sure. At the risk of being irreverent, it could very well be that some pope or cardinal suffered from a chronic cold or hay fever and it saved him from searching through all those vestments, wasting time in search for a handkerchief.

As you might suspect, a pope or cardinal wouldn't have had just a plain handkerchief. It must have been embellished with a few frills. A kind of strap was attached, so it wouldn't fall off or blow away on windy days. The handkerchief itself came to be called a maniple, from the Latin word "manus," which means "hand," to signify that it was close by and readily available.

The vestment must have met with approval and perhaps appealed to other church authorities, especially those who lived in damp climates and suffered from sniffles. As one might guess, especially if one is a Catholic, wearing a maniple eventually became mandatory. It was a rule, and the priest was not considered properly dressed for ceremonies if the maniple was missing. If a priest deliberately excluded the maniple from his regular vestiture, it was considered an infraction of reasonable tradition and, therefore, sinful. This is a long distance from simply wanting to wipe one's nose.

Admittedly, such an example shouldn't be taken too seriously. But it points up the fact that rules and traditions often come about in strange ways. And it's as good a way as any to introduce a very important part of my story — Assistants.

In some ways, assistants are like maniples. No one knows exactly how they came about. It seems reasonable that some pastor somewhere once said: "I can't do all this work myself. I need help." Such a reaction would have been natural, considering all the activity normally taking place in a parish: counseling, teaching, visiting, assisting, participating in ceremonies of various sorts, confessions, annointing the sick, studying, reading, preaching, attending meetings, dealing with the problems of administration, financial responsibilities, keeping a record of most of these pursuits and trying to smile through it all.

Obviously enough, pastors have always needed help. What remains a puzzle is how the priests who helped them came to be called assistants. How did that word develop? In the same way as maniple, I suppose. Perhaps someone started using the word because it gave the impression that the pastor was still very much in charge and that the assistants were called upon to do what the pastor absolutely could not.

Somewhere, recently, the need for a better word has been acknowledged. You don't hear "assistant" any more. It has been replaced with "associate" or "co-pastor." That sounds a little better, more like a sharing and willing participation in the work of the parish.

Until recently, however, it was "assistant." During my tenure, dozens of them were here, of every kind. It would be impossible to remember them all. Some remained only a short time. Some came so long ago, they offer only a vague memory. It would be an injustice to treat them only generally, so I leave it to you, reading this, to conclude that they were good, willing, making every effort to sustain their sometimes impossible tasks, crying more than they laughed, often taking life too seriously and not seeing the better side of their efforts. It is my thinking that priests do some of their best and noblest work as assistants. They are worth remembering.

Willie was like most pastors where assistants were concerned. He saw them as a kind of personal property. It isn't that he wasn't kind to them and sensitive to their position. He was attuned to the drama of unfolding events in their lives.

The situation of any priest was something of a scenario in itself. After ordination, the usual first step was to become an assistant, unless the bishop had something else in mind like studying more, or doing office work connected with administration (a fate for many worse than being assigned to the most belligerent pastor). Being an assistant meant one worked "under" a pastor, who was the authority in everything — what the meals might be, what time the assistant should come in at night, when he might take a day off. He could tell his assistant what to say in a sermon, what projects to undertake, and might tell him what to wear on certain occasions, or send him on the most menial of errands like delivering a cake to a friend or dropping off a personal note to a parishioner. The pastor was in charge. There was no questioning his motives or choice of methods.

Pastors were powerful in those earlier days, in Willie's time. My understanding is that this isn't so true any more. What with liberation and forward thinking, most assistants are braver, more assertive than in those early times. One hears rumors these days about pastors actually being a little afraid of their assistants who insist on inalienable rights, come and go as they please and have whatever they choose for breakfast. It's not the same anymore, I hear.

There are many old stories about pastors from times past which illustrate their authority and power. I remember one about an assistant who came to his first assignment with high expectation and hope. The pastor received him graciously enough and welcomed his presence at the rectory. After the first evening meal the housekeeper served, with accustomed flouish, dessert consisting of preserved peaches and ginger snaps. The assistant, thin and ascetic from years of seminary diet and study, happily prepared to reap the reward for that work and discipline. He helped himself generously to a bowl of peaches and a handful of ginger snaps.

The old pastor stopped his quick hand in mid-air. "You can have either the peaches or the ginger snaps," he said, "but not both."

The assistant, in the strict tradition of obedience, did as told. Later, relating this incredible story to another assistant (for a league of holy association existed among them), he expressed his amazement, overwhelmed that two men, both with at least twenty years of education, mature adults, could so blindly consent to act in their given manners. The assistant voiced to his friend those resentments which he deeply wished he could have presented to his pastor. But, of course, he couldn't or wouldn't, for lack of courage and the ever-pervasive presence of fear. He lived bravely in that situation for almost seven years, eating ginger snaps or peaches, or whatever new choices might come, but never two together.

The story should end there, but, as in all true stories, it only began there. Eventually that assistant became a pastor, taking scrupulous care never to delineate between the choices of desserts. He made an effort to serve sometimes three or four desserts. No penury here. Let's have a generous approach.

But he did insist that his assistants not use the parlor to receive their friends. Let them accommodate their companions in the offices provided. The parlor was strictly reserved for the pastor's family and close associates. Further, a simple rule (of which he asked rigid observance): no one was to be invited to the house on Sundays, since that day was designated for entertaining those chosen by the pastor. And just one additional, easy rule: the assistants must be present when the pastor had his parents for dinner on Christmas and similar holidays and they should appear in formal dress, including clean cassocks and french cuffs, please. They could be excused later, after the pastor's festivities. He felt it was his prerogative to issue such commands. After all, he was pastor. If any justification were remotely required, he could remember those former days when he had forgone ginger snaps for peaches or peaches for ginger snaps.

A tradition of strength and duration is as difficult to end as it is to begin. Willie was a pastor. That meant certain conditions would inevitably prevail. Assistants knew that. They didn't always like it, but learned to live with it the best they could. They built their own subtle defenses against such monolithic power and depended on each other for support.

It was more difficult when there was only one assistant. Where there were two or more, they could lean on each other, talk it over, nurse mutual ill feelings and hurts. Sometimes they came for a visit, to talk, say a few harsh words in secret, then straighten their shoulders for more to come.

Opportunities periodically arose when the assistants here had a chance for relaxation and careless abandon. Sometimes Willie went away for a time. The assistants, during those rare and welcome intervals, laughed much more freely, resorted to the earthier personal self residing within them and enjoyed, temporarily, a much more mundane lifestyle. They might order pizza, which Willie hated, for every meal and drink beer at the table, a custom without precedent or approval. There were problems of course, even then. No one could ever say for certain when Willie would return. He prided himself on never taking a vacation, a real one for fun and abandon. He always had a holy purpose for leaving: to visit a nun somewhere, see a parishioner in prison or make a retreat.

Sometimes he'd simply walk into the middle of a disorderly situation, unannounced, when every light in the house was ablaze, the radio echoed raucous music and visitors were present. Willie didn't mean to dampen the atmosphere, but he did, of course. He was the pastor and it somehow befell pastors to keep order and tradition.

Some recollections seem highly irregular in my memory, but I am positive they are objective. Two assistants here would run recklessly through the house blowing a duck call and a police whistle as soon as Willie left. Whenever these queer sounds emanated from the doors and windows of the otherwise dignified rectory, neighbors immediately surmised that Willie had gone again. They raised their eyebrows a bit, thinking about grown men and all, but perhaps understood, or wanted to. As you might suspect, Willie found out about it from Alice, his secretary, who innocently asked him why they always did that when he went away. When he inquired about it, tentatively at least for Willie, the assistants demurred and looked, as assistants are adept at doing, as though they didn't understand. Could it be the secretary was mistaken? Had she heard something on the television in one of the rooms upstairs? But in his heart, Willie knew, and accepted it as one of the irritating burdens of being a pastor.

For all the abrasions and tensions natural to the lives of assistants and pastors in their encounters and adjustments toward one another, a certain benefit arose from their association. Even with the unequal level of power, priests in general had no other way of maintaining some semblance of balance. There was no one else to tell them that they needed improvement, needed to grow in their care of others for a more effective ministry. Parishioners wouldn't say much by way of criticism, however justified they might have been. Perhaps they lacked the courage. The prevailing tradition was one of respect and a certain fear of priests. This may not be so much the case any more. It was then. A priest was set apart. He wasn't readily subjected to disapproval or disfavor. He was a priest. The very term explained everything. Further questions or comments were not necessary.

In reality, only priests could speak directly and honestly to other priests. Even then, their admonitions were best couched in terms of humor and subtle innuendo. Taking all this into account, truly healthy exchanges could only be shared by equals — assistants to assistants and pastors to pastors. Undoubtedly the same held true for bishops. There wasn't any serious crossing over, at least from those who occupied lesser positions. True, pastors could demand that assistants shower only in the morning after nine because doing it at other times bothered the housekeeper who lived below; or order them never to enter the kitchen because it was "off limits." Assistants, on the other hand, didn't enjoy the privilege of similar freedom of expression. It was a tradition.

I've known a fair amount of priests in my day, more assistants than pastors. Most of them have ranged from normal to, understandably, just a bit off center. I would be the first to admit that some were regrettably immature, lacked judgment in affairs of duty and application. But most grew in wisdom and even an acceptable amount of grace.

As I've mentioned, I knew some better than others and therefore a few stand out more prominently in my memory. I thought a few might never learn, some who got off to less-than-smooth beginnings. One in particular was possessed with satisfactory good will, intelligent enough, but somehow lacked any accurate perception of the routine and ordinary demands of a parish. His first week was something of a hallmark here. People talked about what happened for years and remarked often that there would never be another assistant like him.

Willie had an extremely specific notion about assistants, a

tightly knit definition of their duties in the parish. His expectations were high, perhaps because he saw service and parish function as the only real priority in his life. It was extremely difficult for him to conceive that other matters such as days off, vacations and even family ties could interfere with the functions of the parish and the individual needs of parishioners.

When that new assistant arrived, Willile approached his initiation with the same dependable enthusiasm he had shown toward other assistants who had served there. He took him hurriedly around the rectory and church, detailing duties and expectations as they went along. What he said only served to constitute a confused haze in the mind of this newcomer. He was in a state of semishock and only answered reflexively, wanting to store the overload of information in his memory for future reference. They hurriedly crossed the street to the convent where he introduced the nuns. It all happened so quickly, with so many instructions along the way, that the assistant retained little more than a blur. If he had wondered about the school and why they hadn't visited it, since he would be teaching there and should know where it was, it didn't enter his conscious mind. Too many details for so short a time.

The next day was Saturday, the beginning of that weekly frenetic rush which the assistant would come to know so well: confessions, evening masses, the Sunday crunch, running incessantly from one activity to another, the demanding expenditure of nervous energy. By Sunday evening the assistant was overwhelmed with it all and felt he had been through several weeks in just two days. Whatever Willie had told him during the initial tour was by now so entangled in an inextricable mass of thoughts and fantasies that he hardly knew what was real. For some inexplicable reason, he was limping, as though he had lost the full capacity of his legs.

Willie, of course, took note of all this and made a rigorous effort to appear fresh and ready for any eventuality — a sick call, Sunday evening visitation at the hospital, come what may. It was a ploy, innocent to a degree, but with its own purpose of motivation: an indication that much would be expected of any assistant who came to work here.

A further gesture, adding to the impression that energy and dedication were essential to any assistant's life, came in the subtle innuendo that there was more to come tomorrow and shouldn't the assistant take the night off, go home, visit his family, rest up a little? Willie would be more than happy to take the duties of the parish. Tomorrow was another day.

The assistant, however doubtful about his role here, gratefully took Willie's advice and went home to watch television with his parents. His dazed state subsided perceptibly and by ten o'clock he felt some motivation to return to the scene of battle, albeit reluctantly.

Returning, he found a note (the first in a succession of hundreds) from the pastor. It was simple and direct, signed with that flourish that would become so familiar to him over the next ten years. It read succinctly: "Father, 6:30 Oblige, WMH."

The assistant probed his agenda of instructions and admonitions to discern, if possible, the meaning of such a cryptic message. He began to experience again that queasy insecurity which had washed over him at the end of the weekend miasma. What did the note mean? There were two weekday masses, 6:30 and 7:30 each morning. This note must indicate that Willie would take the 6:30 and he the 7:30. Was Willie still rendering compassion for what the assistant had endured through the endless weekend? Apparently. Perhaps life would evolve more satisfactorily than he had previously surmised.

Sleeping blissfully at 6:25 the following morning, he was wakened by insistent knocking (more like banging) on his door. When he roused enough to respond, Willie boomed the amazing information that the assistant was due to say mass in five minutes.

One marks life by beginnings, the dramatic intrusion of unseen events which change us and never leave us the same again. The assistant said later, in prayer, that this had been just such an occasion. He remarked that Freud, the father of psychology, had claimed that what happens to one in the first six years of life is by far the most important; that we spend the rest of our existence dealing with what took place in these early years. But the assistant contended from that day forward that what happened to him in the first three days of his career at St. Philomena's would have given Freud cause for revising his assertions and perhaps writing a new book.

He bolted from bed, skipped everything but the barest necessities of biology and dress, and shot down the stairs on a dead run to the church.

You must understand that punctuality is as important a Catholic virtue as any that exists. Masses must start and end on time. Never be late for an appointment. Supper begins immediately at six. "What time do you have? My watch must be thirty seconds slow." "Let's hurry now, so we can begin on time."

The assistant thought he might avoid the ineradicable stigma of being late, the lifetime blight of rejection and disdain, if he could just get to the altar on time. He rushed into the sacristy and went straight to the vesting cabinet. Fine so far, everything in its appointed place — amice, alb, cincture, stole, maniple and chasuble. From there he leaped to the cupboard where the chalices were kept under lock. Key first. Upper lefthand drawer. He inserted it quickly, turned and adroitly pulled the door open.

His instructions for preparing to say mass hadn't included information on an alarm system which should be turned off before the cabinet door was opened. This simple oversight set off a shrill bell which rang stridently in the church, over at the house and, for all he knew, at the local police station.

I remember well that one of the altar boys, David, said laconically, "You have to turn off the alarm." The assistant of course did so but only after alerting the gathered congregation that they might have gotten less than they deserved in this new assistant. But they were a tolerant group and certainly would not reject anyone on the basis of one or two negligible mistakes.

In cases such as these, embarrassing and humiliating as they might be, one only carries on, makes the best of it and hopes to smile a little through it all. The mass was a few minutes late, but not irreparably. All went well up to the offertory when the assistant remembered, too late now, that he was to bring wine from the house when coming to say mass. Why such a perverse procedure? Why not keep the wine in church? An irrelevant question at this point. Perhaps there was a history of bibbers in this church, sacristans, janitors and even an occasional altar boy, God forbid! No matter, the reality was, simply, the wine was still in the house.

What to do? He'd try to catch the eye of Stella, lost in prayer and oblivious to this appalling plight, and signal the catastrophe. Finally Stella heaved up from her personal pew (third row back, gospel side) and lumbered off, none too hurriedly, as though all this had happened before, leaving us waiting expectantly.

What had begun as a bad dream changed to a nightmare. What else could go awry? Nothing, until the last blessing, during which the assistant happened to look down to discover he had the chasuble on backward, cross and gold emblems in front, plain black in back.

There was nothing to do but finish, however dismally, and take refuge by sneaking to the house by the back door. Admittedly, it was a questionable beginning. Surely tomorrow would be better, maybe even the rest of the day.

But it wasn't. In the middle of breakfast, Willie rushed in. In what he regarded as justifiable intonation, he vehemently demanded to know why the nuns hadn't yet been taken to school. He added irritably, "If there is one character I demand in my assistants, Father, it is punctuality."

It was the purest of news to the assistant that his job description included taking the nuns to school. He was by now in a state of near loss of reality, gripping his chair and waiting desperately for that ubiquitous haze, which had its tenacious hold of him once again, to clear. Added to this humiliation and dim vagueness, he had to ask, tentatively and in a barely audible voice: "Where is the school?"

Willie had reached a point of exasperation, but something, perhaps the beleaguered look on the assistant's face, held him in check. He was basically kind and had a sense of conviction that it was not the time for further explosion. He simply said:

"Get in your car and follow me."

The assistant, of course, complied and trailed closely behind Willie as he drove from the parking lot to the convent. When the nuns boarded, they proceeded to the school, six blocks away, a shocking revelation to the assistant. In that short trip there were hasty greetings and the repetition of those wishes for happiness and success which had been expressed at their first meeting. The nuns happily left him sitting limply in his car, waiting desultorily, long after they had entered the building.

In such awkward conditions, there is a point at which reason gently takes its quiet exit. Reasonably, the assistant should have gone home. Unreasonably, he was still bent on following Willie wherever he went, which on that morning was not back to the rectory but on some further errand. After a few blocks, Willie noticed in the rear view mirror that his new and none-too-stable companion was still following closely behind, a few feet from his bumper. There was in the look of the assistant a determination to follow Willie for the rest of the day. At the risk of personal jeopardy, Willie came suddenly to a complete stop, opened his door and with patient deliberation walked back to the assistant's trembling car. He leaned down compassionately, in full view, making sure to articulate slowly for complete comprehension, and said: "Go home," which the assistant gratefully did.

Somehow he felt it wasn't really home to which he was returning. It was, rather, the house assigned to him by those erstwhile forces of fate. Home was a long way from that place, another house, somewhere he had not yet determined. It would be a long time before he could remotely call this residence home. In some senses, as with all assistants, he would never call it home, his home, his hearth of peace and tranquility.

The saving feature of the life of every assistant was, of course, the people. The people out there in the pews, in welcoming homes, at meetings and gatherings. The people who offered the hand of comfort and a word of welcome, who never judged harshly, who took the stranger in and asked so little in return: a kind word in the confessional, a decent sermon, a warm hand in time of travail, sensitive response to the demand of suffering and need. Except for the people, this new assistant, and most of the rest, might not have found home, a haven of refuge. But the people were there. They smiled and offered the hand of hospitality.

I hear much has changed in modern times. Priests sometimes live apart now, each in his own apartment, or in different parts of the house with little or no real contact. I wouldn't construe that I am qualified to say anything about that, certainly not to pass any judgments. I just have my own experiences to remember. I'm sure the lives of the priests who were here could have been better. Some have alleged that it was an abnormal way to live, those men together by decision and consent which were not their own. Probably most of them wouldn't have chosen those particular persons as their daily company. Today's approach might be healthier. Who knows?

I appreciated and welcomed the assistants who became part of life here. Even churches have natural preferences. But not one of them who came had any but the best of intentions when they came. All wanted to do something noble. Many of them, for whatever reason, fell short of what they had anticipated. Perhaps a little more encouragement, acceptance, and trust would have done some of them a great deal of good. Who knows? Perhaps the people could have had a little more to say about them, what they had to offer and what they were asking of them. If the people could have offered their assistance, I might still be standing today, still putting my arms around the parishioners. I'd like that. But I'm not bitter, not angry. Some things you can't take away. I'm glad for life. And I know all those assistants were a part of that.

Chapter Five

THE MARVEL OF REMEMBERING

Sunday ceremony offers undeniable drama. There's a certain completion to life there with the church filled to the rafters, all the noise and excitement, and goings in and out most of the day. I always thought Easter and Christmas were wonderfully stimulating, though I harbored some persistent resentment toward all those nameless faces I never got to see for another six months or a year.

After all these years, the history of my full and phenomenal life, when I think of it on those days when I'm feeling bright and able to reason clearly, I've seen a prodigious number of people. I know it's ridiculous, but I think of most of them as my family. You might laugh, but I secretly used to call them my children. That could have been because many of them did childish things when they came.

Sometimes, if it was cold and snowing outside, they tracked in mud and ice, crumpled up their inexhaustible supply of Kleenex and left a mess. It's surprising what you see after a major liturgical affair and a veritable deluge of visitors: old gloves which never match, letters to friends, chewed-on pencils, a plethora of used hankies and similar useless materials. Once someone left a pair of shoes (some bride or groom who wasn't thinking clearly). They tell me people called the rectory regularly asking about purses and billfolds, keys, a child's left mitten, even wristwatches and earrings.

Dogs sometimes came in for a look around, mostly on spring or summer days when some fresh air buff left all my doors open. I remember once when a kindly looking pooch came in during the middle of a sermon. God knows, it's hard enough to listen to sermons, no matter how good, Sunday after Sunday. I've heard them on just about every subject imaginable, from Creation to the Last Judgment. When a dog saunters blithely in, it constitutes, for most preachers, an insurmountable obstacle. The best of preachers must throw in the sponge.

Well, this dog walked right in and, contrary to the inclination of most Sunday attendants, ambled directly up front and assumed its accustomed canine stance. Facing the preacher squarely, the pooch looked at him complacently. Some of the congregation, inclined to a touch of cynicism, said the dog seemed more interested in the sermon than most of the people. You can take that as you like. Others, whose acrimony ran more deeply, speculated that God had appeared before in the form of animals, and might have been in that dog, come to assess our devotion and attentiveness.

It looked like any other dog to me, a black and white mix with a too-long pink tongue hanging out the side of its slack mouth. But still, no one could say for sure and perhaps was thinking about that passage from St. Paul which suggests that God has appeared in many ways.

In any case, you can understand something of the feelings of the priest giving the sermon. He was just getting started and was always a little tense while preaching. Sometimes he hurried, rushed right along. Most of the people didn't know exactly why and used to talk about it. But I knew. Stella told me one day during prayer. She said he was dreading the possibility that Willie would show up, listen to what he was saying and then give a class that evening on better techniques of preaching. Not that he minded the classes, it was just that they always lasted a long time, with an unusual amount of repetition. Just when he thought Willie had ended his remarks, he would suddenly offer a further point. This sometimes went on until late, dimming the possibility of going out to dinner or home to visit the family.

What does one do in the middle of a sermon with a dog in the center aisle? The people had ceased listening. The ushers were showing signs of life in the back. They stopped talking and riveted their attention on the dog. Maybe they thought of asking the dog to leave, but it was a big dog, seemingly friendly enough, but who knows what a dog might do? Once during a Tuesday night novena, an apparently harmless canine sneaked inobtrusively in, hunkered under the pews, got a bit confused and started barking, right in the middle of the third joyful mystery of the rosary. Everything stopped right there. We just couldn't go on. The barking got louder with the poor dog not knowing how he got there or how to leave. One of the braver ushers crawled in after him and made a grab for his paw. What could the usher expect? The dog bit him on the thumb and retreated a little deeper under the pews. Amidst all that anxiety, with everyone telling everyone to stand back and cautioning that the dog might be dangerous, with the usher holding his thumb and thinking about rabies, a little girl crawled to the dog, made a few friendly sounds and led it outside. We weren't sure what Hail Mary we were on, so we started the third joyful mystery over again.

So, you see, we knew about dogs, the priest and I. We'd been there before. It was then that the priest got what he later assessed as a flash of genius. He knew he'd lost the day to the dog. Why go on? So he said to the congregation, "If that dog isn't Catholic, it'll have to leave. If it is, will one of the ushers please find a seat for it."

Just about everybody started laughing. Sort of low at first, because laughing wasn't fully approved of in those days. Then the dog sat up to attention, expressed its own understanding by barking loudly, stood and wagged its tail.

The people roared. I think it was just then that they got the idea that God was actually appearing in that dog. "At least it could have been St. Francis," some of them said, and started laughing all over again.

Of course, not everybody laughed. Some failed to see the humor in it, thought the priest was a coward for not putting the dog out himself. The priest, however, thought his remark was funny enough and laughed right along with the people. But through it all, there was that little dark cloud of doubt which often came over him at times like these, when life should have been happy. The priest knew that Willie would hear about the whole affair. Maybe already someone was rushing over to tell him. Maybe Willie was in the sacristy right now, looking between the cracks in the door.

Happily, nothing ever came of it. When the priest walked over to pray that afternoon, he told me that everything was normal so far. If Willie did hear about it, he wasn't saying anything. He could have been saving it up, to get it out with a few more serious sins, like the week before when the lights were left on all night. But to that point, it all seemed secure enough and the priest felt optimistic.

I just can't help emphasizing that people are interesting. I loved my people, my family, and thought they were the best ever. Sometimes I heard about new churches going up somewhere around town. There were stories of stained glass from Munich and wood carvings from Trent or Bolzano. I'd never heard of some of the furnishing which graced other churches: scamnum, balachinos, apses, naves and transepts. Here, we had only pews, the middle aisle and the main altar. We only heard at a distance about carrara marble or Hamburg pipe organs. It never seemed very important to me. I had long contended that it is less what is inside a church that is important than what is inside the people who go there. Someone once said in a sermon, "Wherever people are, there God is doing wonderful things." I believe that is true. Wonderful things happened here, not just once in a while, but regularly. Granted, we were human enough and God at times might have been taxed more than usual in bringing out wonderful things in us. But here we were, sometimes rough, but there all the same.

Take our ceremonies, for example. There wasn't a church anywhere that did them the way we did. Some might have had more appealing vestments, larger candlesticks, more vigil lights, sweeter incense, but I always describe our ceremonies as unique.

In the first place, no two were alike. They had a charming variety and spontaneity not found in other places. The ritual of holy week this year was no guarantee it would be the same next year. Solemn high masses with priest, deacon and sub-deacon, were as changeable as the seasons themselves. Even each daily mass had its own flavor.

If you ask why this was, most would heartily agree that Willie was principally responsible. In addition, it was quite natural for the rest of us to follow along, he being who he was, his singular persuasion in the lives of so many people. As far as we were concerned, the Second Vatican Council brought the rest of the Catholic Church to where we already were. Certainly in spirit.

Willie could preach on a moment's notice. He had so many sermons inside of him that at least one was always available to fit the occasion. Sometimes a thought would strike him like a voice from above and he'd be swept completely into the subject for fifteen minutes at least, maybe a half hour. He loved to make announcements and hardly ever looked at the Sunday bulletin before hand. It was his time to bring us up to date, a kind of oral newsletter: who was sick, who died, where he'd been the past week.

He might tell us about someone who was married on Saturday and we'd be graciously informed of the family's history, the bride's parents and ancestors, who came to Denver first, what they did, a recounting of their accomplishments. In some circles this might have been less than tasteful. Here, though, we knew Willie and where his heart was and gave our tacit permission for such renditions.

Actually, no one ever knew for certain what was coming. Certainly the priests didn't, let alone the people. With the respect due to the revered memory of someone as imposing as Willie, I'm not sure that even Willie knew. But it didn't seem to bother him. He took seriously the admonition of Jesus about not fretting over what to say and that in the moment of need the Spirit would prompt those who preach the word. He loved it and felt as at home at the pulpit as anywhere.

Preaching was simple for him. He relished it, thrived on being able to turn phrases, rise to the drama of it all and mesmerize a congregation. For other priests who came here, it was not always so easy but sometimes the bane of their existence and a heavy burden. One priest confessed in prayer that it was the most difficult fifteen minutes of his week. He maintained that preaching might have been all right if one were called upon to give his best effort once in a lifetime. Perhaps even once a year one could rise to the occasion and offer something arresting and unforgettable. But it is the rare expert indeed, he maintained, who can leave his listeners limp with submission, rigid in the pew and asking for more week after week.

Sometimes, late at night, when I knew no one else was coming, when the doors were locked and only the vigil lights were winking, I got to thinking. As near as I could calculate, Jesus gave three, maybe four sermons in his life. There was the one on the mountain and several minor and shorter talks back in his home town. I think the sermon at the Last Supper might have been considered major, among the very top. Other than that, there weren't too many of what we'd call formal addresses. He certainly didn't preach every Sunday at, say, five or six masses. Sermons weren't the essential effort in the life of Jesus that they are for priests today. He was a good speaker, obviously. The Scripture is filled with what he said and how convincing he was. He had an uncanny capacity for saying just the correct word at the proper moment. A lot of priests have been here, wishing and praying they could do it half as well.

I've always had sympathy for priests who didn't have a natural gift for preaching. I tried to hint to Willie that he shouldn't have been so hard on some of his assistants when it came to preaching. But Willie came from a different age, one where preaching long and sometimes deeply intellectual sermons was as important as any concern in the Church. Willie was a master at it. He had the voice, the gestures, the shaking fist and quavering tone to fit and give harmony to any emotion. Granted, he got a bit brittle in his old age and at times rambled a bit, but he was effective to the very last.

All of life was something of a sermon to Willie. He was always preaching. Some of the other priests who slipped in to pray told me that he preached to anyone who would listen. He even preached when they didn't want to listen. He couldn't help it. It was as much a part of him as his mind, his arms and hands.

If someone came to the house to fix something or put in a new fixture, it was likely that some kind of a sermon would be part of the experience. Stella used to say he was the best there was. She once told me he was born to preach and she couldn't imagine a time, even in his childhood, that he wasn't holding forth about something.

I felt a certain sadness toward the end of Willie's life. He still had something of the old glowing coals in him, but found it more difficult to maintain some kind of order over it all. Sometimes he'd begin a story which would remind him of another, which, right in the middle of the second, would remind him of a third. I sometimes would count and wait for him to come back and finish them all. If he ended most of them, left only one, or perhaps two, out there dangling and unfinished, I thought it was above average. I didn't think it was old age particularly. He just had so much on his mind he couldn't get everything in.

Sometimes we had visitors who were great preachers. They prided themselves in their ability to shake people from their complacent satisfaction. The best preachers came when we had missions and retreats. They were here a week or two, offered their best, and were off to other parishes. When Willie came in for a visit at night, he might mention in prayer that he didn't think those preachers were that great, certainly no greater than he was. Was he a little jealous? I can't say. I'd never think anything that harsh about Willie. He was too good to me. I think Willie knew those preachers had a lot of time to polish their sermons, go over them minutely and make them the best.

I remember once hearing one of them give a sermon on the Mass. It was flawless, rich in imagery, impeccable in delivery, smooth and without the slightest hesitation in search of words or expression. Afterward, one of the assistants was offering his personal accolade. "It was the best I've ever heard," he said. "I'd give anything to be able to preach like that." The preacher stood and took it all in with appropriate modesty and I thought I detected a tinge of blushing. He humbly offered his gratitude and accepted the neophyte's encomium. I was touched.

As they were preparing to leave the sacristy, a woman came in and joined their conversation. "Father, I enjoyed your sermon even more this time. I heard you give it twenty-five years ago in Chicago and want you to know that it was instrumental in my conversion to Catholicism."

That's when I learned the meaning of "pregnant pause," which is what ensued and convinced me that any one of the assistants here could have done a creditable job if he had twenty-five years to prepare for it.

All that might be by way of saying that I heard any number of fine sermons over the years. What impressed me most was that everyone tried, did the best they could. For some, it was less than others. They all wanted to give what they had.

There are so many incidents I remember about preaching, and about ceremonies we used to have. Once it was one of the assistant's turn to preach. That particular assistant lived and worked here for over twenty years. Preaching wasn't his strongest attribute and, now that he is in heaven and these revelations don't matter so much, I can tell you that he took most of his sermons from a book. In those early days, and perhaps even now, books were published with sermons for every Sunday and holy day. All the preacher had to do was read them, word for word, from the pulpit. If he had plenty of time, he could type one out ahead and give the impression he was reading his own sermon. If he was pressed, he could cut the pages out, the way this assistant did, mostly. That was the best he could do, because he wasn't much of a preacher, as I've mentioned. He had other qualities to make up for it. He was gentle, and never got really angry at anyone. Another assistant was fond of saying that he'd lived with him for eleven years and never had an argument. He was just that way. He'd take early mass, hear confessions at school, take communion calls, do just about anything and always cheerfully. But he couldn't preach.

On one occasion Willie told the assistant that he would make the announcements at Sunday mass and afterward the assistant could preach. When the time came for announcements, after what seemed a longish pause, and with some embarrassment, the assistant didn't know what to do. He knew the parishioners had plans for after mass — ballgames, mountain trips or maybe they were hungry and thinking about going out to eat afterward. But Willie did not appear to make announcements. Finally, the assistant reasoned that Willie could as easily make them after the sermon as well as before. Willie probably was delayed somehow. So Jim gave, or better, read, his sermon, word for word, right off the page. He finished and still Willie didn't appear. So he sat down and said an Our Father or two, hoping Willie would show up before too long.

After what seemed an interminable period, Willie walked in with a flourish and treated us all to the news of what was going on and the important events upcoming. When he finished, he turned toward the assistant and whispered audibly, "You can preach now."

Jim whispered back, less audibly, perhaps from respect, that he had already given his sermon. Now in situations like this one, Willie had the modest fault of not listening very closely and so he repeated his demand that the assistant get on with his sermon and not waste time. By now the assistant was a little nervous, not being extremely comfortable with Willie anyway. He kept thinking of all those people out there, waiting for something to happen. He wanted to assure Willie he had already preached, but he was afraid that he might get into some undignified shouting right there on the altar. Maybe, too, by this time (though he never told me it was so) Jim may have begun to feel just a bit perverse over it all, seen a little humor and irony in the situation.

So, much to the surprise of everybody there, the assistant sauntered over to the pulpit, slowly, for effect I thought, picked up his sermon and read it again, word for word, every syllable.

What was most amazing about it was there wasn't a sound; no one laughed, no one jumped to shout, "We've heard that one before." I like to think it was all out of sympathy and understanding for the assistant, although I don't know for sure. More cynical folks remarked that no one paid attention to sermons anymore and this proved it. That might be true.

Once someone related a story about a priest who offered the same story for three weeks running, at all the masses. A courageous lady came up after mass and brought this to the priest's attention. "Did you know that you have been giving the same sermon for three weeks?" she asked with just a tinge of haughty irritation. "Yes," the preacher replied with unruffled confidence. "Do you mind if I ask why?" a little more stridently now. "No, indeed. When you all start doing what I've recommended in that one, I'll give you another."

I keep thinking of all that has happened and all that should be remembered. Someone said that history is a way of learning, helping us not to repeat our mistakes and hoping to remember the good we have done. I think that's true. History is so important. Even the history of a little church, torn down and forgotten, where only weeds and a little new asphalt replace the majesty and dignity of a building. I miss it all. I miss it too much.

In all my history, stretching back to 1911, there is such a variety of events to remember: two world wars, a series of smaller ones, and all sort of meaningless. Freedom and justice are no nearer than when it all began. All those desired ends, equality and freedom, peace and tranquility, seem sometimes remoter now than when I was born. In those earlier days life seemed so simple, less frantic than now. We talk in terms of progress, and I suppose we've made some, but it seems as though we have a long distance to go.

Learning and awareness, however, come eventually to those who are open and willing to progress. I remember that we had a visiting priest one Sunday to help out. He was young and taught at a local college. No one ever really knew what visitors were going to say and there was no way of checking before hand. I had the impression most times that people held their breath and hoped that visitors wouldn't dislocate their faith too much and that they would say something both informative and at least a little entertaining. It seemed reasonable to me that such humble anticipations were little enough to ask.

On this particular occasion in the early 1960's, our visitor began talking about the war we were currently fighting in Viet Nam. He said, to our chagrin and surprise, that we shouldn't be in that country at all, and that what we were doing there would sit heavily on our conscience for years to come. He said, further, that we ought to be writing our president, our senators and representatives about stopping that war and letting people live in peace. As if such surprising recommendations were not enough, he expressed his conviction that even Communists were human beings, and might not be as bad as they were made out to be. He said we were killing innocent women, children and old folks who didn't even know what the word "Communist" meant. Our eager willingness to root out the political evils in Viet Nam needed more prudence and humility.

Well, we all gawked and gaped in disbelief. I know I did. We were of a different mind, had been brought up to believe our country and its leaders couldn't make mistakes. They had the right to do what they wanted and the U.S.A. was the most powerful country in the world.

Our visitor finished mass and was scheduled to celebrate one more that Sunday. He had hardly left the altar when some of the people streamed out of church and went immediately to the rectory to tell the assistant, who told Willie, who came downstairs in a righteous fit of indignation. Willie was a true American. His background was one of patriotism and deep fidelity, never mind these young leftists who were exhorting rebellion and insubordination.

Most of us thought Willie was absolutely right. But I did feel a bit sorry for the young priest. He seemed so mild and took it all in good grace. Willie insisted that he say the next mass without preaching. One of the assistants was enlisted for the homily. I can't remember for certain but I have the recollection, however dramatic, that the sermon was on loving your enemies and doing good to those who persecute you. It was delivered well enough and the parishioners attending that mass simply took it in stride, thinking our visitor wasn't feeling well or had a long day ahead of him.

I often wonder what happened to that young priest. What he

said was the beginning of what others would be saying more and more as time went on. Even bishops here and there began to say the same thing, even some politicians. I think you could say that the war in Viet Nam eventually stopped, not because we won, not because we proved we were right, but because most people were ashamed of the killing and the terror. It is a paradox when I think of that young priest, that he turned out to be right when we all thought he was absolutely wrong.

Willie is in heaven now and I'm sure that issues are clearer for him. If that priest ever wanted to talk about what happened there so long ago, I'm sure almost everybody would be willing to apologize. I know I would. Those were hard times.

There were other times just as difficult, such as the second world war when so many left homes and families, when some never came back. We kept a list of all who went, and a special list of those who didn't return. We hoped that it would all stop with the end of that war. We know it didn't, but we're still hoping.

I have just one more story to tell about preaching. It has to do with a service on Holy Thursday. Holy Week is a special period and brings lots of added tension for priests. There's so much rush and hurry, getting it all accomplished, ending up in a state of exhaustion by Easter. In those early days, the frenetic state of things was even more confusing than it is today. Ceremonies were more complex, more detailed, and there was the need to do it all in Latin. There was singing and preaching, long lines for confessions, services packed with people, getting ready for the final drama of Easter Sunday. It was an occasion of sincere conversion for some. Good intentions ran high. Those who had been absent for a time readily accepted the twinges of guilt for not having done better since last Easter. Resolutions of all kinds were undertaken. There was a unique joy in the sheer good feeling of telling God of one's willingness to be back among the faithful and the sense of cleansing which is welcome when new resolutions are made.

The priests always saw Holy Week and Easter from a little different viewpoint, like a deluge of too many demands in too short a time. They heard confessions for hours, attended ceremonies at the Cathedral, tried to fit in visits to the sick and shutins, and to find some of the feeling of the season besides. So they were busy and, understandably, a little harried, sometimes a bit testy. The worst personal confrontations came at Easter and Christmas, times when one would think things ought to be better. You could expect it as sure as the moon's rising. Sometime before the final day there would be dissatisfactions and the exchange of ungraceful remarks over what later seemed innocuous and inconsequential. Easter and Christmas were the best of times and the worst.

On this particular Holy Thursday the mass had begun. Willie was the celebrant, the two assistants were deacon and sub-deacon. It was a most solemn occasion, one which the people in those days attended religiously, so the church was filled. Willie intoned the Gloria in Excelsis Deo, a traditional and auspicious prayer, the last vestige of joy before Good Friday. The priests then sat down while the choir began to tread its way through the poliphony and cadence of its selected rendition, offering their very best and culminating a long series of rehearsals during the months before.

The priests were just settling down when Willie turned to one of the assistants and said, "What are you preaching on?" To appreciate the impact of Willie's question, you'd have to know that assistant. It was the first time he'd heard that he was preaching that day. He wasn't the most secure person in the world and life, most times, was something of a blur for him. With all sorts of happenings taking place around him, he seemed to be outside most of it. Because he was young and new as a priest, he was just learning to survive. His morning prayer, which I heard many times, was simply one which asked that he get through the day. He didn't see himself in light of what he could do, but only what he had to do.

So when Willie asked, "What are you preaching on?", it staggered him. The blood rushed quickly to his head making him queasy and faint. He thought of telling Willie he was sick, which wasn't by any means inaccurate. He thought of running out of church and explaining later. But he lacked the courage.

He could only say weakly, "I thought you were preaching," and that in a very respectful tone.

In former times, Willie might have risen to the occasion, walked to the pulpit without hesitation and delivered one of his historical half-hour sermons. Now he was getting old and wasn't up to it, so he simply said, "No, you are." With that terse phrase, the matter was settled.

What was the assistant to do on Holy Thursday, one of the most imposing days of the church year, when many who hadn't been at church for a long time and those who had, were expecting something worth hearing? How do you preach when you've got the rest of the Gloria, the epistle and gospel — about five minutes in all, to prepare?

That was a memorable day. The assistant didn't do badly, considering. Basically, I would say he started with the beginning of creation and went forward. He looked at his watch several times and when he got to about fifteen minutes he wound down, perhaps somewhat abruptly, and finished. It wasn't the best, but it wasn't the worst either.

The people? Well they were accustomed to such events. They never knew for sure what was going to happen and at least some of them came for that reason. It gave them something to talk about. At another mass when Willie happened to be deacon, he remembered he had promised to take Communion to Mrs. Witashek. He loudly proclaimed so to the priest and the congregation, promising to be right back and advising everyone to continue without him. Compared to such surprising episodes as this, a rambling and faintly related sermon was comfortably acceptable.

I miss it, I must say. I'd give anything to hear a sermon of any kind, prepared or not, just once more, in the building I used to be. I have some pleasant memories. If I'm quiet, settle back and catch the spirit of it all, I can still hear them, see the people, get the warmth of it all. It's a comfortable feeling.

Chapter Six

PASSING THE BASKET

I don't think Jesus ever took a collection. I suppose some astute scripture scholar could make a case for such, as they do just about anything. But I, with admittedly limited background, have never found evidence of it.

I do remember that passage in which Jesus and his small group didn't have any money to pay some tax or other. In the midst of the confusion Jesus directed one of the apostles to go down to the shore of the sea and catch a fish. Afterward, he looked into the fish's mouth and found a coin sufficient to satisfy the tax collector. What an impressive gesture. I've never heard of a pastor who did anything remotely similar.

Certainly Willie didn't have that sort of power. It might be true that most pastors are skeptical of the literal truth of such a story and would settle for the symbolisms involved, pointing out that the writer of the gospel wanted merely to say that, if we trust, everything will be all right.

In a remote passage in scripture Jesus exhorts the disciples to go out and preach the good news. It is a totally amazing fact that Jesus admonishes the disciples to take along nothing that will burden them or hinder their progress in any way. He specifically dictates that they should not take money, extra clothing, shoes or emergency provisions. Willie loved the scriptures, was thought by many to be something of an expert in their regard, but he always thought that kind of thinking (I mean about having no extra money to take care of things) changed when they built the first church in the early centuries of Christianity. It wasn't that he doubted what Jesus said. It was simply a matter of practical deliberation. He used to say the disciples didn't have to worry about light and heat bills, assume responsibility for upkeep and offer a generally good image to the people.

So Willie, as any other pastor, saw collections and such as essential ingredients of the parish. Much of his time was preoccupied with ruminating about how to motivate the parshioners, how to keep the parish in fiscal balance and solvency. I would never describe him as avaricious. His personal life was extremely simple. As I said, he gave away most of his own money and had no notion of aggrandizing bank accounts and escrow. He simply knew that any parish required money and ongoing support. He had a theory, however, which he expounded to asistants: it is always beneficial for any parish to be "just a little" in debt. Not too much, mind you, but enough to remind the parishioners that they are encouraged to be generous.

You can understand, then, that the Sunday collection was always an important event. Churches and church life naturally acquire a certain measure of ritual, and the collection was no exception. Assistants were given specific instructions about how the money was to be taken to the house immediately after mass and counted, and that caution was to be taken for maximum efficiency.

Every assistant participated in this ritual of helping to count the collection, tally it and ready it for the bank. No one was to schedule other duties during this time. Death, sickness, or catastrophe took second place to the collection. It was all a part of total ministry. No one joked about it, at least within Willie's hearing. It was a grave business which couldn't be fully appreciated by those who were not responsible for paying the bills.

In all my history as a church I've never known anyone who was fond of collections. To begin, there are too many. Whoever originally thought of them is traditionally recognized as a genius. Church lore has it that collections were originally composed of food and goods, to be used at the pastor's discretion for the needs of the people. Parishioners brought, say, a sack of wheat or a bushel of apples, some corn or other useable material from their provisions. As parishes grew in size and complexity, methods of sustaining their needs changed. The collection of goods was gradually replaced with donations of money, a better medium for the purposes which had come into being with the development of the parish.

Historically, the person who thought of collections, admittedly a genius, has become secondary to the person who hit upon the idea of second collections. It is my humble conjecture that the creator of second collections will one day be canonized.

As I've said, no one likes collections. However, most agree that they are necessary. I would be hesitant to admit it publicly, but the most impassioned pleas I've heard in my time were for money. I've never been privileged to watch television, but I'm told that those Sunday morning preachers are far superior to anything I've ever witnessed. I can't see how that could be, after all I've heard. They say a bit of haranguing, a little pressure in the right places, makes some people feel just fine, motivates them, and offers a sense of satisfaction when they do give.

For all that, I would say most people don't particularly incline to sermons on money. Any parish has a ledger of individuals who leave because they've heard one sermon too many on generous giving. Add to that the flux of those who arrive because they have left some other parish over the repeated talk there about money. People were always coming and going, or had ceased coming at all. I've heard more than one individual whisper in the confessional that they'd been away from church for years because they left in disillusionment when some priest ranted and besieged them about the collection.

Willie never did that, not to any abusive extent. He sometimes thought he was going to and would work up his courage during the week and tell the assistants to get ready for an impassioned plea. Then, by the time Sunday arrived, having visualized the faces of the people who would come to church, seeing elderly ladies, favorite members who had been more than responsive in the past, he'd offer a few cursory thoughts on generosity, not even very specific, and hope for the best.

My recollection is that the people here were very generous. They responded readily enough and the bills were always paid on time. I think Willie worried excessively over debts and such, sometimes to the point of panic. It was true, as in most parishes, that support here came from only a portion of the members. Those members loved Willie and would have accomplished just about anything he asked of them. Periodically, parishioners stopped by the rectory or dropped envelopes in the mail with extraordinary assistance, beyond the bounds of justice and charity.

Permit me to return to second collections for just a minute. The truth is that nobody, not even pastors, and certainly not Willie, had much affection for them. He used to complain they were an impediment to effective administration. If you announced a second collection ahead of time, parishioners offered less in the first one. If it wasn't announced, they felt they had been deceived and resented it. He complained that he had no control over most second collections and that he was forced to take them simply because the bishop or someone "down there" told him he must.

In addition to those "official appeals," there were always others. Missionaries traveling through asked for assistance, as did various groups doing special work, and just about anyone who had a project that needed money. It seemed less than human not to respond to all of these needs. The people complained sometimes and whispered to one another about too many entreaties and when would it all cease? But still they gave.

Every parish uses methods in addition to the collection for financial support. There are always yearly projects and objectives to sustain ongoing demands such as bazaars and bingos, campaigns and drives, raffles and drawings, sales and boosters. These undertakings are as much a part of a parish as weekly mass and Saturday confessions. Willie didn't believe strongly in most of these, at least not deep in his heart. As with his initial fervor over sermons on giving, he could become highly charged over a bazaar or a drive to raise capital funds, then he would falter, and, in the end, tell the people not to give more than they could afford and thank them profusely for their generosity.

Another avenue of survival for most pastors comes from the few individuals in the parish who are blessed with wealth. Some of them can't be approached and quickly offer excuses about not being able to give at the moment, but be sure to call later. Willie came to know that sort quickly and saved energy by not repeating his appeals to them. He knew that the parish was supported mostly by those members who were just getting by and didn't have any outstanding money in the bank.

There are in almost every parish, however, a few individuals who are extremely generous. These dependable patrons are not inclined to dramatic ostentation. They don't ring bells and form a procession when they give readily. They quietly offer amazing assistance. Most pastors want to be careful about these willing sources and let them make their own studied decisions.

I remember once when Willie left on a trip — not a genuine vacation because, as I've mentioned, he was hesitant to call his departures vacations. This time he planned to see some Sisters in a nearby city. The assistants knew from past experience that he might return at a moment's notice. Sometimes he turned around to come home before arriving at his destination.

This is exactly what happened on that occasion. He came home almost immediately. Willie rushed excitedly into the house, giving every evidence that he had conceived an idea worth pursuing. He called for a meeting and presented an inspired plan to the assistants.

He'd been thinking about the school, he said, offering that cryptic beginning as an indication that he was about to expatiate to some fuller and fantastic plan. That small building was becoming a bit cramped and could benefit handsomely from the addition of a few extra classrooms, a meeting room, and a hall that could double as a gymnasium and multi-purpose room. He'd calculated some, pondered the situation, and estimated that he could accomplish that whole project for around a hundred thousand dollars. He knew that he couldn't sustain such a large debt because the Archbishop would never approve. What about asking Rick, a faithful parishioner of generous and sensitive nature, for the money? He had been speculating that Rick just might respond and offer support for such an idea.

The assistants knew Rick and had made their greetings and sensitive expressions to him whenever he came to church, which wasn't often because he was frequently out of town. Willie knew him best and was in the most advantageous position to approach him. Did the assistants think it wise to pursue such a daring objective? They did, obviously because Willie did, and it was expedient to concur in such ponderous matters. Assistants rarely thought of disagreeing. When they did, it was more often after the conversation had ended. Imagine disagreeing when Willie was worked up that way and plunging forward recklessly.

So Willie unfolded his scheme to the assistants. He would write a letter to their wealthy friend, explain the matter of the school and how he conceived it should be expanded, ask please if Rick were interested in assisting in the project, leaving latitude of course for whatever dissent Rick might wish to express. If he felt he could make a contribution it was certain other members of the parish would follow his excellent example and give what they could, just as he had. Of course, they all recognized his many obligations, that he was limited like everyone, and would understand if he demurred. However, they were encouraged by the fact that he had been extremely generous in the past, which gave them hope that he would support this one more project which would benefit so many, stretching beyond them into the future for generations to come.

Willie was a gifted letter writer, especially when it came to making delicate appeals. They were sometimes a bit dramatic and hyper-extended, and made people smile. But they were sincere and well meant. I'm sure Rick chuckled a bit when he eventually received Willie's letter, seeing all those superlatives and that gracious wording. But he had read those notes from Willie before and knew he had a good heart. He was convinced that Willie was ever a gentleman.

They didn't send the letter immediately. Willie set to work writing it, then rewrote it, then started over again. The assistants thought it might never be finished, thought Willie would flag and lose heart in the interim. As in all situations like this one, I watched through my windows to his. The lights stayed on late that night. When they finally blinked off and darkness swept over the rectory, I was just beginning to believe Willie had finished the letter when suddenly they would come on again. He must have changed the wording and syntax several times during that night.

It was said later that Willie decided not to send the letter. He somehow began to worry that Rick might not take it kindly, might think he was being importunate and reject such crass boldness. Better to abandon the project than offend his friend. The assistants knew this was a fragile time and they didn't want to express any untoward opinions. From experience they knew Willie would spend the day making and rejecting his decision several times. They offered reassurance in soft phrases such as, "Whatever you decide," and other non-committal assents.

By evening another draft, this one final, was composed. It consisted of several pages and said almost exactly what the first one did, but everyone felt better about it because it gave them, especially Willie, the comfort of knowing he had worked very hard and struggled to make the letter gracious and dignified.

The posting of such an unprecedented appeal was awesome. Willie couldn't just put it in the mail like any other letter. It seemed that something more should be done, some further step, perhaps a ceremony or liturgy of some kind.

In the end, everyone in the house — assistants, housekeeper and secretaries — proceeded to the church. There they deposited that auspicious letter on top of the altar, then knelt down and prayed privately. Communal and spontaneous prayer were little known in those days and still something of a cause for personal embarrassment. The prayers were sincere, however, each different, all with the same plea: "Oh God, let our friend read this letter at a good time, like after breakfast in the morning, or in the evening at the cocktail hour. Thank you. Amen. And, of course, let his response be favorable."

They left the letter there overnight to bask in the winking comfort of vigil lights, in the presence of the gathered saints, in the house of the Lord.

I read the letter in the quiet of midnight and found it entirely plausible and certainly within the bounds of legitimate petitions. It contained a certain calm demeanor, assurance of understanding and gratitude whatever Rick's answer might be. There was, finally, a sure promise that Willie had not undertaken this rash venture without sufficient consideration and stress. Only in light of the possible wondrous outcome had he been able, even remotely, to contemplate such radical thinking. There followed the accustomed assurance of sincerity and fond greetings. It was signed, "Your Humble Servant."

Willie came early to retrieve the letter and it was posted that morning. Nothing now but to wait, which everyone did as the first week slipped into the second and then into the third.

Willie began to suffer those misgivings which were so typical of him, speculating and ruminating over his lack of sensitivity and urbanity. It was characteristic of him to remonstrate over his compulsive nature. Why had he done it? He agonized over the impulse to pick up the phone, call Rick and apologize for his pretentious behavior.

The assistants, being less involved emotionally and having learned from past events to take such anxieties more calmly, blandly placed it all in the hands of God and went about their duties. If hard-pressed, they might have admitted that they had all but forgotten about it, or at least had relegated their concern to the remoter labyrinths of their minds. Not Willie. He simmered in concern and self-doubt. With the passage of each day, hope ebbed that some graceful conclusion would be reached to end his increasing anxiety. Perhaps, perforce, he ceased thinking about it himself, if only to save his frayed spirit.

Late one evening, around nine, a man rang the bell at the rectory. Ruth, a faithful evening receptionist, answered the door. When the visitor inquired if the Monsignor were home, Ruth made a hasty and protective judgment, answering that he was not in, when, actually, he was upstairs. In her estimation, he was tired and in no condition to see casual callers at that hour of the night. Nonplussed, the caller asked if she wouldn't deliver an envelope to him at her convenience. She assented, accepted the envelope politely, and, seeing no reason to invite him in, bade him a good evening.

Ruth went immediately to Willie's "hook," a place for messages and reminders, and attached the envelope to a clipboard there. She treated the entire issue with customary aplomb, feeling she was doing her very best as a receptionist and friend of Willie. She was, of course. Ruth loved Willie with a fondness and devotion seldom found in this vale.

Late the next morning, as Willie was passing the board, he noticed the envelope, picked it up absently and proceeded to his room.

Sometimes, if the mood prompted him, if he was weary and listless, he'd intentionally pass that board by and ignore the notes and scrawlings there until the time he might feel more inclined to the duties inherent in those messages. He got to his room and might have laid the envelope on his desk. Whatever the case, he eventually opened it. It contained two simple sheets. The first, a letter, was written in longhand, short and immediately direct. The second was a certificate transferring shares of stock in a prominent national firm worth some ninety thousand dollars. The letter stated tersely that its writer apologized for the lack of more immediate response, but he had been out of town and only recently returned. It went on to say that he hoped the enclosure might assist in the project outlined in Willie's letter. He was grateful for the opportunity of assisting and glad that Monsignor felt comfortable enough to ask.

Well! Willie prided himself on his calm demeanor. He lost control at times, but never voluntarily. One seldom, if ever, saw him jump or shout out those expletives to which most resort when excitement takes hold. He wasn't without emotion, but it came controlled, well organized, with a broad smile, a florid compliment (and a few tears when others were unaware).

That morning Willie bordered on some visible sign that he was extremely excited when he read the note and saw the certificate of stock. He ran from his room and began to talk to anyone within hearing, which surely covered a radius of three or four blocks. I certainly heard every word he uttered. He covered over some of his enthusiasm by demanding to know who had received the envelope and so carelessly left it unattended at his clipboard. Fortunately for the assistants, they were guiltless of such an egregious breach of courtesy, not inviting the benefactor in and offering hospitality. One of the assistants was only able to relate that Ruth, just prior to leaving the night before, had mentioned that someone had brought a letter by for Monsignor and she left it on the hook. There was nothing over obvious about such happenings, since many people were rather consistently coming to the rectory with a note or a greeting or an invitation.

No one knows how Ruth defended her behavior. Perhaps she merely pleaded ignorance. I suspect that, in the rush of joy and triumph, she was rather easily exonerated that evening. All ended well. That night the lights blinked out at their appointed time and I had the impression that my companions were sleeping the sleep of peace. Money does make strange creatures of us all.

What else can I say about passing the basket? Not much, really. It was passed often and filled repeatedly, not with magnanimous amounts from accrued stock and liquid earnings, but equally generously, with those smaller amounts which admit a largess comparable to the widow's mite. Contributions came not from abundance but from little, garnered carefully and portioned out scrupulously to a long list of needs, including the church. There is nowhere greater benevolence than here, a kindness and trust that the "church" and the staff there deserve it. It offers a challenge to be met, repaying that deep confidence and faith.

True, large and surprising donations were welcome occasions for amazement, fostered talk about God's smiling approval of a pastor here, a church there. But, for simple financial security, there is nothing like the dependable Sunday contribution of good parishioners. Every pastor knows this and struggles to walk a line between pleasing the community and not diminishing his effectiveness as a conscientious minister. It has often been said that the collection is an accurate barometer of the people's appreciation, or lack of same, of the pastor, the staff and what is taking place in the parish.

I always judged that we were doing fine here. Most parishioners seemed to be happy and willing to signal their satisfaction in many ways. There were a few obvious exceptions. A few wanted shorter sermons, faster masses, a getting on with it so they could start the next activity in their lives. Others wanted extra masses, added at more convenient times, such as four in the morning during the fishing season, or eight at night for skiers. That number was small, though vocal.

Throughout our colorful history, with many assistants coming and going, transitions in the church in liturgy and ceremony, different bishops, a host of parishioners moving in and out, the collection was stable and grew with the cost of living. It is true that many members who gave a dollar a week in, say, 1935 were still giving the same amount in 1975. Many others, however, were conscientious. They took their responsibility very seriously and compensated for those who were less generous.

If the measure of satisfaction was the Sunday collection, there was a short period when we all thought disaster had struck. The assistants who counted the collection noticed a marked reduction in loose bills, especially larger ones. Every pastor wants to encourage parishioners to use envelopes and speaks eloquently of business-like organization, easier records and immediate verification for tax purposes. Be all that as it may, there always remains a number of reluctant members who refuse to be convinced of the need for envelopes. They simply prefer their way and refuse to be convinced otherwise.

Whatever was happening in our midst, something was dramatically awry. Where were the large bills? Why was the collection up to a hundred dollars short of previous Sundays? This was a case for pondering, calling for more than cursory investigation. It happened, at the time, that we were blessed with an assistant who was "ideal" for this pursuit. He readily volunteered to "take the case" and Willie offered his ready consent.

Of course, I knew what was happening, but couldn't say

because communication between a church building and human beings is accomplished only by the power of unspoken suggestion. When the assistant taking on the role of detective came into church, I began concentrating on thoughts which, I hoped, would move him in directions that would lead him to startling discoveries. It might be that this assistant thought that he was operating independently, but that simply was not the case. This problem might never have been solved had I left him to his own resources. It is quite possible that he would have missed completely that which was most obvious in the case.

Our hero kept his ear to the ground, questioned trusted people subtly and surreptitiously. He asked if anyone noticed anyone not contributing to the collection who had in the past. Such investigations led to no conclusions and frequent assessments of other possibilities.

Then one Sunday morning the assistant noticed something extremely significant that led, eventually, to the solution of this mystery. He saw one of the ushers, basket in hand, head toward the stairway to the choir loft which always harbored a few parishioners who delighted in taking refuge there rather than mingling with the rest of the community. The assistant roughly calculated the time lapse before the usher's reappearance. He noted that the basket was passed last in that lofty place, after having wended its way among the parishioners in the body of the church.

What was happening in that interim? Our detective said nothing and continued for a week to nurture his secret thinking. He went several times to the choir stairway and clocked his time from bottom to top and down again. He estimated the time by counting to himself and was satisfied that he could produce an accurate measurement.

The following Sunday our detective slipped stealthily toward the back of the church. The usher taking the collection ushered at that mass regularly and always took the basket up to the loft. Sherlock, which is what I was calling him by now, did his calculations and was again satisfied that there was an obvious discrepancy in time. He was ready to make his move.

A few more discreet inquiries revealed that the usher in question for months had been taking the collection at that mass, the 11:15, well-attended by generous contributors. For months, almost every Sunday, he had ascended to the choir loft with the collection basket. The pieces were fitting and Sherlock was ready to conclude his case.

It came the following Sunday. Standing quietly in the shadow at the back of the confessional, Sherlock waited. When the usher entered the choir loft door, Sherlock slipped quickly to the staircase and stood excitedly beside the baptismal font so as not to be seen. When the usher reappeared, he descended quickly to the middle landing where he stopped and began quickly to stuff bills from the basket into the pockets of his jacket. I remember well the tense look of abandon on the usher's face as he worked quickly to scoop from the collection basket any loose currency.

Precisely at that moment Sherlock stepped from the lower section of the stairway and moved quickly up the few steps which separated him from the usher. He hadn't ascended half of them when the misguided thief uttered a low gasp of panic in recognition and horror. The bills were in his pockets, the basket irreversibly in his hand.The assistant said very little and, knowing Willie wouldn't tolerate any dramatic tactics, he simply informed the unfortunate culprit that he would see him after mass.The usher said nothing as his oblique eyes flickered with vague assent.

After the mass the usher was taken before Willie who was obviously shocked and incredulous. He might have said a word or two in reproof, but he certainly wasn't going to press charges or be vindictive. I can't tell you exactly what transpired, but I suspect that Willie asked a few questions, perhaps upbraided the usher's conduct. Knowing Willie, he might have ended by offering the culprit assistance for whatever was motivating him to steal money from the collection. Of course he wasn't to usher any more and no one would know why unless the usher himself chose to tell.

Sherlock felt he had done a needed service. He rated himself a sleuth and couldn't resist talking about it a bit. Those who knew him, though, were accustomed to taking what he said with a grain of salt.

The case thus was solved quietly, without undue humiliation or retribution. The collection regained its healthier status. The assistants returned to more concerted concentration on Sunday's game and the usual trade in desultory conversation while processing the Sunday's proceeds.

Need I say more about passing the basket, other than it was passed often and always received by the members of the parish with generosity and grace. It has been going on for centuries, this hallowed custom which speaks to the virtue and kindness of those who come to church. They take their place in the long line of the many who have gone before to offer support and service.

Chapter Seven

BLESS ME FATHER FOR I HAVE SINNED

Willie loved to tell stories about priests from the past, their marvelous feats and accomplishments. I had the impression that he thought the Church was better for their pioneering spirit. He said that, in those days, there was more of a sense of adventure and forging ahead to the frontiers of faith and mission. He relished the memories of priests who were remembered for what they did. They lived on in their reputations by what they left behind in exciting, colorful legend. Sometimes he expressed disappointment in modern ministry, where priests may be cut from the same mold and rest in pallid hues of neutrality, as contrasted with those out of a more adventuresome and risk-filled time.

Willie recounted some of the same stories over and over, taking care to get them exactly right, faithful to detail and circumstance. I must have heard some of them a dozen times. They drifted lazily into my hearing from the dining room on summer evenings. Sometimes I'd hear them from the sacristy where Willie talked occasionally in good humor to one of the assistants.

He once related the experience of a pastor, long dead, who remained in vivid memory because of his liberal spirit and forceful style. An elderly woman approached him in a fit of depression and anxiety. Her husband, a "good man," had dropped away from the faith many years before. He hadn't been in a church for years and sometimes chided his wife for her faithful attendance at mass and devotions. He laughed, even made harsh jokes about her piety, about faithful parishioners and especially about the priests, telling her she ought to see through those "fakers" who talked too much about money, lived better than most people in the parish and walked around like they knew everything.

As the story unfolded, Willie told how the poor woman related that her husband had become very sick. The doctors said it wouldn't be long before he died. The woman cried as she expressed her deepening concern for the poor man. What if he should die without the sacraments? What if he wouldn't have the opportunity of going to confession? The time was growing short and could the pastor help her? It wasn't as though her husband was bad or sinful. They'd raised several children. He'd been liked by his friends. He was kind enough. Sometimes he helped those in need, even secretly and without fanfare. Once he'd lent some money to another couple who suddenly found themselves without enough money to survive. There was just this one obvious fault, his rejection of the Church, his apostasy.

He hadn't always been against the church and religion. When first married, they attended mass regularly together, never missed a Sunday. He was what people sometimes call a "model" Catholic. He belonged to the men's club, contributed to the weekly collection and even helped some around the parish.

For all that, though, he had always been a little skeptical and sometimes talked irreverently about the priests, saying they were a bit too "holy" for him and why didn't they have a few of the problems he had if they wanted to do all that preaching at him?

For some reason, he stopped attending church after going to confession one Saturday afternoon. He never mentioned what had happened. His wife probed a little, offering gentle inquiry at first, but he refused to discuss it. After a time she simply dropped it, not wanting to make him angry. He never went to church again, not even on Christmas or Easter, not even when the grandchildren were baptized or made their first communion.

Well, what she hoped the priest might do (and she knew it was a lot to ask) was to visit her husband, just drop by because he'd heard he was sick and was there anything he could do? Perhaps her husband wouldn't respond the first time. It was, in fact, highly unlikely. After a second or third visit, however,

71

he could bring up the idea of confession and getting his life in order before death came. Of course, he didn't have to put it that way. Priests were better at knowing what to say than she was. She had faith that he could do it if he would just be patient enough to get through the initial meeting.

As Willie related these details, he chuckled again because he wanted to assure his hearers that the priest in question didn't require near that much encouragement. He had a wealth of experience in these affairs and looked on this situation as a golden opportunity. He assured the woman he'd be at their home that afternoon. She was somewhat surprised at his quick response, thinking he might have said he'd be there next week, or, at least, in a day or two. She said something about going right home and getting ready, thanked him for his kindness and hurried away to tidy up the house and say a few prayers for his success.

Willie went on to explain that the priest in question was an extraordinary figure among the people of his day. He had a finely honed sense of the trials and problems of the average parishioner and the benefit of broad experience. He had lived for a time in the mountains where he ministered to many people scattered over a wide area. He traveled from one place to another on horseback and by train. Once the train he was riding derailed, turning over the engine and pinning the engineer under the wreckage. The passengers were urged to leave the train quickly and stay at a safe distance because the boiler could explode at any moment. The priest wouldn't listen. He crawled under the engine to talk to the trapped engineer who, it turned out, was a Catholic.

While the engine emitted a foreboding hiss, threatening to explode at any second, while everyone shouted at the priest to get out from under the engine, the priest and the engineer talked. He heard the man's confession, assured him that everything was all right, that he was at peace with God.

Eventually the priest crawled out, much to the relief of the gathered onlookers who were standing at least 150 yards away. The engine never did explode. The fire in its boiler gradually went out, but the engineer died before they could bring help. Both his legs were caught under the weight of the wreckage and his body was so bruised that he couldn't last. He just stopped breathing.

Willie always interjected this story within the story to build up the dramatic ending he was about to reveal. He used the word "rough" to describe his hero, not in the sense that other people use it but to give an idea of how hardened to suffering and pain he was and how a priest in those days had to be tougher than they were later when conditions became "modern and soft."

Returning to the story of the woman and her husband, Willie told how the priest arrived at their home that very afternoon, as he had promised. The woman thought the priest might pretend that he just happened to be passing by and was there anything he could do for them. Not this priest. He began immediately to tell the sick man how his wife had come to him, told him her husband was sick and that the doctors were concerned; told him how he hadn't been to church in a long while, that it was time for him to come back to the good graces of God, and he'd come to hear his confession.

You can imagine how surprised that poor man was. He was polite enough, not in the mood to quarrel but adamant about not needing the priest's services and certainly didn't want to go to confession. This didn't stop the priest. On the contrary, it seemed to fuel his fervor. He became more insistent, reminding the man that he wasn't going to live forever and they could do this in just a few minutes. Again, the man courteously refused. The priest once more insisted.

How long this went on no one could say for sure. It was obvious that the priest wasn't going to leave and equally apparent that the poor sick man wasn't going to go to confession. Finally, in a fit of angry desperation (and you'll have to forgive him for this) the priest shouted, "God dammit, get on your knees and go to confession."

There was a moment of silence. The only sound was a partially suppressed gasp of horror from the sick man's wife. The silence protracted into the brink of eternity. The priest apparently sensed that he had gone too far and looked a bit sheepish.

Willie was faithful to minute detail at this point, assuring his gaping listeners that the priest had related everything to him later. I had heard the story so many times before that I knew it practically by heart. I was always amazed at his return to the same words and even the same inflection in his voice when he said "God dammit," and then paused for the effect on his listeners. Relishing the shadow of scandal the story offered, he related the consequences of the priest's careless expletive.

It was in that awkward and intolerable silence that the priest began to take stock of what he had done. In a far less strident tone, mollified by his own arrogance, he reminded the sick man that we all sin and that is what confession is for. He promised he'd mention using the name of God the next time he himself went to confession and said such language was the bane of his existence. No matter how hard he tried, it came out unexpectedly in the most unforeseen circumstances. He was sorry and he'd try harder to curb this capricious habit. Obviously he was deeply embarrassed and wanted to make amends.

The sick man sat for a long time, looking obliquely at the priest. Finally he smiled, just a bit at first, then broadly. The priest looked confused and chagrined. Then he began to smile himself, as though he were comfortable in the knowledge that he had been something of a fool. The man asked his wife to leave for a few minutes so he could go to confession. She did, joyfully and completely mystified by the strange ways of God.

What the man confessed no one, of course, knows. He lived only for a few months and the priest saw and talked with him regularly. He brought him communion and anointed him with the sacrament of the sick. The priest was not there when the sick man died but his wife assured him that it was peaceful enough with no extraordinary struggle or resistance. The priest wept some over the loss of one who had so shortly come to understand him and remarked later that he received something from the sick man that he had wanted for most of his life, a sense of acceptance and tolerance for his weaknesses. He said that such regard was mutual.

The past twenty-five years or so have witnessed the advent of newer and clearer theology. Much has been said and written about confession and its place in the lives of Catholics. Some theologians would maintain that both the sick man and the engineer who died in the train accident didn't really need confession. They were both good men, intended to do what was right and never really rejected God. Who would hold their human failings against them for all eternity? I would tend to agree but something can certainly be said about how confession helped both of them by giving them a sense of security. It isn't so much that they had to go to confession but more the idea that they both gained something for themselves by that act. It gave them the opportunity of saying they were human like everyone else. It offered the chance of hearing another human being, the priest, assure them that it was alright, that's the way life is, a kind of dance with sin in which one can finally say, "For what is incomplete in me I am sorry."

I recall other stories that make the same point, that people need to feel they are forgiven. I remember a young priest who was returning to Denver on a plane. It was night and all the passengers were asleep or quietly resting. The lights were off in the cabin and the steady drone of the motors was the only sound. Unobtrusively, a stewardess sat down beside him and whispered that they were having some difficulty. An instrument was malfunctioning and there was the distinct possibility they'd have to land without benefit of the wheels, skidding clumsily onto the runway on the plane's belly.

The stewardess asked quietly if the priest could hear her confession. She whispered all this in the lowest possible tone because she didn't want anyone else to know the situation just in case the pilots got it fixed and they wouldn't have to announce the emergency after all.

The priest fought down that rising panic which invariably accompanies such circumstances. He admitted later that he began thinking more about himself than the young woman who wanted to confess her sins. He said, making some attempt at humor in that grave situation, "I'll hear your confession if you'll hear mine right afterward." Even as he said it, he became aware that he was much more serious than he'd intended to be. As much as she, he needed to hear someone say that his shortsighted and imperfect life was understood and tolerated by someone, even this stranger who sat in fear beside him. He never finished this story and didn't reveal whether he'd actually made his confession to the young woman or not. I somehow think that he did. I've always maintained that it is in just these situations that we find God best, in each other and our willingness to do what we know God would do at that moment.

I remember another story about a priest who went to an ice skating party with some of the members of his parish. It was a cold night, bright sky overhead and music drifting across the scene. There were sandwiches and hot chocolate, a warm fire inside. The priest was enjoying himself when a young girl skated up beside him and put her hand comfortably in his. He was flattered and began to relish her company, more than he knew he should. They exchanged a bit of small talk, skated around the rink a time or two when she asked, without missing a push or glide, if he would hear her confession. It seemed just the right time for it all and she'd been thinking about it for a long time.

Almost before he could answer she said in a modulated tone, coming somewhere near the droning most people use in the confessional, "Bless me father for I have sinned," then enumerated her various faults and shortcomings. She finished quickly and was given a penance and forgiveness. When all was over, she let go of the priest's hand and, with an expression of gratitude, gracefully glided away from his startled presence. He was glad for the brief encounter and felt that he was needed. He appreciated the affectionate response so many people held for him.

One absolute conclusion I have reached in my life here is an appreciation of how much time priests used to spend in the confessional. With some contributions from a healthier theology, people are not as inclined to depend on the sacrament of confession the way they used to. Most Catholics have arrived at the conviction that they can trust more fully in God's acceptance and understanding of them. In many respects I think that what is happening today is more realistic, a better approach to the role that forgiveness plays in our lives.

Seeing all the people in the old days flocking to church on Saturday afternoons, standing in long lines and then whispering their little sins to the priest seemed to me a bit overdone sometimes. Some people came every Saturday. You would see them arrive regularly, sometimes before the priest, waiting for him to enter the confessional so they could be absolved again of their sins. It was my studied judgment that there really wasn't that much to absolve. I knew most of them and they weren't what you'd term hardened sinners.

Of course, it would be totally unethical to reveal specific sins or identify the individuals who confessed them, knowing how private confession should be. I can only speak in generalities. I've listened, couldn't help hearing those lists of sins for almost seventy-five years. There are many sins in the world. Some egregious and heinous: murder, treachery, seriously hurting others, psychologically as well as physically. I can candidly assure you that the great majority of people who came here hadn't committed sins of that sort. They were human, like Willie's priest friend who slipped and said "god damit." Oh, occasionally I heard something that might astonish me, but those times were rare. Even then, I knew the penitent wasn't all that bad, after all.

Sometimes I found myself wondering how conditions got to be the way they were, I mean why people thought they had to confess so often. Why did they feel so unworthy, so sinful? I have this recurring hunch that frequent references to sin and how difficult it is to be forgiven are often used to stir up guilt and make most people do just about anything. Because they sometimes suffered from an undue preoccupation with their sins, it happened that the priest or the bishop took advantage of them, made them obey laws and demands which weren't all that necessary for a virtuous life. It is a welcome change in the church that we are thinking about confession and sin in an entirely different way now, speaking of forgiveness in a more positive reference.

Thinking about it all, I've come to the thinking that confession wasn't all bad. It had its bright side. People came to know priests better when they had those heart-to-heart conversations with them in the confessional, however short and simple. I felt that one really knew what a priest was like by the way he heard confessions. Some were too routine and gave the impression they wanted to get it over with as quickly as possible. Others were patient, willing to take a minute to talk and offer a word of advice. Still others reacted as though sins offended them more than they did God, becoming sour and touchy when someone hadn't been to mass or when a young person had a few bad thoughts. It was that kind of priest the people tried to avoid. Sometimes I saw parishioners come in and see that a harsh priest was the only one hearing confessions that day. They'd say a quick prayer, apparently for forgiveness of what they were about to do, and beat a hasty departure without visiting the confessional at all.

Most penitents can tell a horror tale or two about confession. I've heard some affectionate references to confessors, such names as "Dutch Cleanser" or "Old Bismark" (after a Prussian general who was so hard on his soldiers that many of them deserted). Catholics tell about priests who kept them in the confessional for fifteen minutes, lecturing them on some point about sin and its consequences. They relate stories about priests who gave them heavy penances because they happened to follow someone who must have had a lot to say before they got there. Sometimes individual confessors grew worse as the day wore on. If you wanted fair treatment you had to get there early. Sadly, it happened at times that people had such negative experiences in the confessional that they stopped going to church altogether. Those are embarrassing tales and shouldn't have ever happened in a church where we want to offer love and forgiveness.

But then there are those who speak in glowing terms of recollections of cherished moments in their experience of confession. They remember for life a word or two of advice or reassurance which was offered to them. Some can recall word for word an inspirational or motivating phrase used in their regard which changed the course of their thinking, made them completely different. Some might have felt such a flush of confidence that they would discontinue a paralyzing weakness once and for all, never to be tempted toward it again.

Most priests spoke about confessions humorously, perhaps the only reasonable way to deal with the topic. They could offer repeated anecdotes about what penitents said. Take children, the ones who said, "My last confession was a week ago. Since then, I've missed mass three times." Sometimes six or seven year olds admitted bravely to committing adultery. Others insisted, "Oh my God I'm partly sorry for my sins," or, better, "I'm hardly sorry." Some wailed in panic when it came their turn. Once a nervous child vomited after laughing uncontrollably for a full minute. It was all in an afternoon's work.

Sometimes elderly people came and, because of the solemn and ominous silence in the confessional, turned their hearing aids up to be sure not to miss what the priest might say. Such actions were signaled by a high pitched whistling which drowned out what the penitent was saying. If the priest was conscientious and new at hearing confessions, he was more prone to ask the penitent to repeat, making some remark like, "What's that?" or "I didn't hear you!" Sometimes there were long pauses, indicating a lack of contact altogether. About the time the priest might give up the effort, the penitent might say, "What's that?" in a totally unconfessional tone. You can imagine the confusion which might ensue. Occasions like these often ended in total chaos, with confessor and penitent shouting at each other such phrases as, "Go ahead and finish now" from the confessor, eliciting disconnected responses like, "How many Our Fathers did you say?"

It was what we have come to call the state of the art. Most priests liked to hear confessions well enough, within reason. On a Saturday, when they heard three or four hours, it wasn't all that difficult. Christmas and Easter were a different story. There was a rush to get to confession. Priests entered the confessional as if sentenced to solitary confinement. They wondered if they might ever finally exit from that dark, uncomfortable cubicle. I remember a priest here once who heard confessions for eleven hours in four languages. He was, of course, fine in English, good enough in Italian and Spanish (except for some esoteric sins which didn't come up often or which penitents used to confuse him) and in German he had to do a copious amount of guessing, leaving the balance to a good and gracious God, who, he trusted, would understand, and who, he suspected, had never intended for anyone to hear confessions for eleven hours in four languages anyway.

Willie always said he liked to hear confessions and that the occasion was an opportune gift for "counseling souls," as he used to put it. Realistically, I think he'd heard enough toward the end of his life and was happy just to turn the whole task over to the assistants. Once in awhile he suffered guilt pangs and renewed his resolution to take his turn with the rest of the priests. This would happen mostly around holidays, when long lines evoked those old stirrings within his pastoral soul. Then he'd do his stint, not in the normal, quiet way, but with the flair and elan that were so characteristic of Willie.

When such enthusiasm was stimulated, he'd wait until the lines were long and people were getting a little restless. He'd come into the church with a flourish, knock heavily on the confessional doors of the assistants who had been hearing for hours, and announce in his deep, dramatic voice, "I'll take over. You may leave." The priests were happy enough to do just that and Willie would hear with a fervor, stepping up the action and buzzing right along.

That sort of approach was a little difficult for some people. Willie knew just about everyone who came to confession, especially those who had been in the parish many years. He might interrupt some faithful parishioner's confession by asking how her mother was feeling or whether she and her husband were planning to attend a given meeting. These asides always shocked penitents, no matter how accustomed they were to Willie. Sometimes they were left speechless and couldn't relate what they'd come to say. The more daring ones attempted to disguise their voices, speaking a little lower or higher. Not many deceived him. Little wonder some people sneaked out when Willie came to do his time in the confessional.

On one such occasion Willie raised a number of eyebrows and drew a loud gasp from an old and reliable parishioner. He made his usual entry, knocking on the confessional doors in his dramatic way and dismissing the assistants. In his peremptory voice he announced to the gathered people that he'd be hearing confessions now and would they all please form a line for his confessional. Well, there were quite a few penitents on that occasion and they began to break from the other lines. Some hesitated a bit, not wanting to go first, hesitant to let Willie know who was coming in. Others knelt down in the pews to re-examine their consciences and say a few more prayers, perhaps for the grace of patience and perseverance. I knew that some of them were going to leave as soon as Willie closed the door to his cubicle.

All that didn't bother Willie at all. To confirm his nonchalance in their presence, he loudly announced to one of the women, "You can go home, Nell. I know what you're going to say anyway."

Nell blanched and attempted some light response by tittering a bit, but I could tell that she was in no condition to go to confession. She stood her ground, though, not to be denied her Christmas duty. If you knew Nell, you could understand and appreciate her determination. Others left hastily, but she stayed. When it came her turn, she peacefully entered. I know there were no sins in Nell's life. She might have confessed something about being uncharitable toward the people who lived downstairs and played loud music all night; or she may have forgotten to say her night prayers once. It could even have been a "heavy" confession, including something about being lazy, sleeping in the previous Sunday and attending the 11:15 mass instead of the 6:30. Nell loved Willie. He'd been extremely kind to her during her years here. He treated her with dignity when others might have passed her by, so she had no trouble forgiving him. She never thought of it again and simply acknowledged, once more, after how many thousands of times, that this was simply another of those puzzling characteristics of the Monsignor.

Actually, I thought confession was a rather enviable act for Catholics. It gave them something others didn't have. I don't mean they should have felt superior about it, looking down on those who didn't go to confession, but it added something to their conviction that sin could be forgiven in a concrete and tangible way. Most people like to know they have been absolved of whatever it is they have done. Somehow, it gives a nuance of official flavor to their lives and adds a little meaning.

I admit readily that some abuses crept into the style of some priests, such as anger and taking forgiveness all too seriously. But most people here had decent experiences. On a given Saturday afternoon those who came went away feeling lighter and somehow renewed by what they had undertaken.

If there are any conclusions which might reasonably be drawn from the subject of confession, the people involved and the disposition of the priests, I would be inclined to maintain that there is one inescapable reality about it all. Stated simply, it is this: People are mostly good, human and frail, but well meaning and offering ample evidence that they intend the best. If you put in a line all who came into St. Philomena's church for confession, it might stretch half way around the earth. It would be composed of a multitude of people of every conceivable class of person. In every instance, at the moment they came in, each of them, without exception, had good intentions and wanted to do better. They confessed their sins and went out resolved to try harder. That's an incredible amount of goodness. It had to have its effect in life and the history of the world.

There are moments when I wonder where they all are. Some of them, of course, are dead. Sadly, some of them have stopped going to church altogether, ceased to see it as necessary. Most all are still trying, resolving to do better, making the best of difficulties, satisfied that they have made some progress.

Does confession make a difference? I can only say it gave most people a chance to look a bit more deeply, to see something in themselves they might have passed over unless they had taken the time to think a little and assess what was happening in their lives.

Once a young woman came to confession here. She was in a quandary over what was happening in her life. It had to do with not being able to control a destructive habit she had acquired. It was causing her deep anguish. She was saddened by her inability, the broken promises so often re-made. As she confessed these things, the priest listened and hoped he might be of some help to her. He had been in that situation before, wanting to say something which would make a difference. He didn't offer anything extraordinary or startling, as though he were the font of great wisdom. He assured her he shared her concern, hoped she might find strength to ameliorate her situation. He made a suggestion or two and gave her the customary penance and absolution.

The priest forgot the incident quickly. How could one remember all those individual confessions? Sometimes he worried about his inability to be more concerned for that long, anonymous line of penitents. For years he remembered going to sleep one morning in the midst of someone's confession. He awakened with a start to silence and the obvious absence of the penitent. She might have told others who were waiting there was no sense going in because the priest was sleeping. He knew who the woman was and wanted to say something afterward but didn't have the courage. The event never really dimmed and kept coming back to haunt him.

Returning to the woman who was so troubled, the priest happened years later to be at some social event. An apparent stranger approached and asked his name. When he responded, she related simply that she had gone to confession to him years before. She thanked him for his kindness on that occasion and related that what he had said had effected a radical change in her life, bringing about the resolution of an overwhelming problem.

The priest, of course, couldn't remember, but he was grateful for her expression. He could almost feel himself sitting in what he and other priests had called "the box," a small, cramped area, a worn chair whose seat was hard and uninviting. He could faintly hear that intense whispering, sense those pungent odors which added a touch of mystery to sin — tobacco breath, the sometimes fresh smell of newly washed clothing complementing the bath of forgiveness that confession was meant to be. Glowing in what this woman had said to him, the priest felt a rush of gratitude that it had happened, that he had been there, a part of the lives of people. Now that he was older, he had the recurring conviction that the people in those long lines had been good, perhaps better than he had been, for all of his so-called holiness and dedication.

I can still see them coming in on Saturday afternoons and evenings, on days before Christmas and Easter. Somehow, though, I remember the afternoons in spring best, when winter was passing and there was a bit of green around the outside, an early flower or two. It seemed so natural at that time of new life, that people would be coming to confession.

I can hear those gentle, whispering voices. "Bless me Father for I have sinned." It seemed so humble, so beautifully human to me. I hear the priests saying, over and over again, without ceasing, without the line ever ending, "Go in peace now, and may God bless you.

Chapter Eight

THE LIVES OF THE SAINTS

Willie hadn't slept well and morning was a long time in coming. It was a weakness of his, if that's what insomnia can be called. Really, it was more akin to an affliction. He couldn't explain it and resented the fact that in those quiet hours, when everything loomed larger for some reason, when others were sleeping so soundly, he was awake, restless, pacing the floor.

Sometimes he'd go down to the kitchen to warm a glass of milk. He had read somewhere that such prescriptions induce sleep. But they didn't for him. It was simply a way to pass time. He could walk a little, clear out those half images which crowded into his mind when he was suspended somewhere between fitful sleep and wakefulness. He disliked the feeling intensely.

On this particular night he'd gone down twice, sorting out the milk carton from other incidental items in the refrigerator — a residue of gathered leavings in jars and dishes which cluttered the shelves and racks. He viewed the confusion with distaste, more so than if it were daytime with the sun shining across the linoleum, evoking a better mood. He thought of speaking to Stella about it. Why didn't she throw half the refrigerator's contents away? What possible use did a bottle of Wishbone dressing, a quarter inch from empty, have? Plastic containers of various sizes held meager leftovers — a half potato from last week's pot roast, several peas, a carrot slice, swimming silently in some nondescript coagulation. How could a body live with so much disarray?

He knew he wouldn't speak to Stella. He had done it before, working up enough lather to confront her, but it did no good. Arguments ensued, anger and the extraction of the grudging promise that she would do a better job in the kitchen, with no manifest improvement. They had argued in the past, sometimes for hours, even the entire day, with what almost seemed agreement to rest between bouts, to gather their respective forces and search out new lines of defense. They had known each other so long, it was almost like not arguing at all, even though their voices assumed the high pitch of resentment, often shouting at each other. They knew they would be forgiving in the end and even depended on these dyspeptic encounters for catharsis and release from tensions they both suffered but never acknowledged. They knew better. Nothing would change. Maybe some minor alterations would take place, but only for a week or two. Then those old habits and quirks of character would subtly creep back. The former, more deeply rooted behavior would prevail.

Willie was older now and had learned that when morning came, when light filtered back into his room it would seep into his soul also and he would be thinking more clearly, with less agitation. He had only to wait for these murky shadows to dissipate with the coming of day. It was a consolation and comforted him as he trudged wearily up the stairs.

But on this morning he had more than the usual difficulty shrugging off that unease the sleepless night had brought. He was tired, more accurately, exhausted. Something was going on which he couldn't quite discern. It happened to him at times — a sense of distress and depression which plagued him for days. Even though he wanted desperately to shake it, he could only partially succeed. It grew in insistence and was there, lurking, even when he busied himself with parish administration, visiting and talking with parishioners. He could stay its arrival for a day or two, sometimes a week. But eventually it demanded recognition, insinuated itself into his thinking, engulfed him.

He dreaded it. He knew that it could only end in hurt and disillusion. He would say or do something which he would eventually regret, have to amend. And as surely as he knew it was about to happen, he was helpless to stem its inevitable finality. He didn't understand it and was angered by his inability to deal more maturely with that mysterious pattern which had taken over in him for many years.

Why was it that he could be so effective and suffer this contradictory direction in his nature? He was sensitive, to a degree at times heroic, with the parishioners. He was tireless in his concern for them, helped them, listened, supported, encouraged and strengthened them. It was said of him that there was nothing he would not do in generosity and kindness. He was aware of what people said of him, that he was without peer as a pastor, was loved, reverenced, respected. He knew literally thousands of people, spoke to them as individuals, and valued them. Sometimes you might hear some say they wished they lived in St. Philomena's parish. They had relatives or friends there and knew how they were treated. Those who met Willie once never forgot him, took something of his person away with them, felt gifted for his kindness to them. Sometimes other pastors made what they thought were humorous remarks about how Willie overdid things, was too extravagant in his praise of the people. For all that, he was sincere, unable to understand some realities in himself which made his life so difficult.

I knew him best of anyone. He had that remarkable gift of saying just whatever was immediately appropriate. Even though people would blush and protest that what he was saying was far from true, it made them feel fine and they resolved to try more to be what Willie said they were.

Willie should have been happy and he was, most times. It was just that there was this other puzzling phenomenon which, try as he might, he couldn't understand. Perhaps if Willie had lived later, during that time when people were more comfortable in speaking of their problems, he might have been comfortable speaking to someone about his problem. I think he sometimes thought he should, and came to the very brink of mentioning his anguish to one or other of the assistants or a neighboring pastor. He never did, though, and I always thought it was because he judged it might be an inexcusable admission of weakness. You see, everyone thought he was nearly perfect, made no mistakes. I think he wanted to tell the people that he was human, had the same weaknesses they did, and more. Somehow, he thought they wouldn't let him, wouldn't believe him. Or, what was worse, he thought they might reject him if he revealed that periodic deterioration in himself, the anomalous feelings and querulous irascibility which sometimes inundated him. He kept those unmanageable feelings deep inside. I might have been the only one who knew them fully. He used to come over to pray about it, look for a solution, especially after it all passed and he was feeling better. But I know those mysterious visitations never really left him. They might have diminished some, later, as he grew older, but essentially they remained with him until the end of his life.

On that particular morning, he came over wearily and prepared to celebrate mass. He knew that he had resisted and fought his unfriendly visitor as well as he could. It was about the middle of Lent and he was surrounded by the reminders of the penitential season. The statues were shrouded in purple, the atmosphere was somber and silent. More parishioners were attending mass during the week and the priests were hearing confessions, distributing communion between masses, working harder, giving sway to the season. Willie thought of all the Lenten seasons in his past and let them coalesce into a disconnected whole. He pondered the phantasms of long lines of people, raised faces, searching eyes, as if chanting in tones of confusion and need. He could hear them in their familiar rote prayers and encantations. "Remember, you are dust and unto dust you shall return." "We adore thee O Christ and we bless thee. Because by the Holy Cross you have redeemed the world." "Bless me Father and help me make a good confession." "Parce Domine. Parce populo tuo." "The fifth station: Jesus meets his afflicted mother."

Such memories merged and separated into those amorphous recollections which sometimes appear out of darkness. The presence of those surreal individuals, appearing and receding into the veil of obscurity, seemed to crowd around Willie. How long had he been a priest? It seemed as though it were all his life. It seemed that the lines of past Lents stretched back in time, without any beginning. It was rather like a circle of events which kept coming round, moving away and returning. He was very tired.

He celebrated mass desultorily, without the familiar quick step and energetic gestures so characteristic of him. Perhaps he'd go back to his room after a cup of coffee, to rest awhile in his reclining chair. He hoped desperately that no one would come for conversation or with those familiar problems which often appear at the end of mass. He suspected that people would be whispering about him not feeling well and that he was working too hard.

He was shedding his vestments when an assistant came tentatively to the sacristy. He wanted to inform Willie, as he might not remember, that he was to give a day of retreat to high school students that day and wouldn't be home until after three. They had talked about it earlier, the assistant said, and had agreed that it would be feasible. The other assistant would cover the later mass, hear confessions until nine and thereby enable him to leave a bit early for the high school.

Willie clenched his teeth as he took the amice from his shoulders and let it fall in a limp pile with the other vestments on the counter. He flared with indignation and asked bluntly if the assistant needed to be reminded that it was Lent, that there was so much to be done in the parish, that he was gone more than any assistant ever had been — teaching, giving retreats, taking work outside the parish. Didn't he know that his first obligation was to the parish here? Wasn't he aware that he had been assigned by the Archbishop for work at St. Philomena's, not in high schools, not giving retreats and certainly not attending every gathering they had down there?

By now, what Willie dreaded was beyond his ability to manage. That strange mixture of confusion and anger had overtaken him to the point where, even as he was regretting what he was saying, there was another strain of compulsion in him which made him feel justified and even righteous over his feelings. He concluded his remonstrations with the acknowledgement that he would be better with one assistant who was content to stay in the parish and work than with two like him, who insisted on traipsing around doing God knows what.

It all ended as quickly as it had begun. The silence followed heavily, then the careful steps of the servers beating a quick exit. The assistant stood silently for a time, then said, practically inaudibly, something about being more careful in taking outside commitments in the future. If Willie had hoped for some reciprocal anger, an attempt on the part of the assistant to justify his behavior, he was disappointed. I think he was secretly thankful that the assistant was so taciturn and compliant. Willie knew that this particular assistant's tactic was not to argue or show the least sign of anger. He preferred to withdraw, say very little and languish in the humiliation of such encounters. He left quietly with no recourse other than to go to the high school, give the day of retreat, however difficult that might now be, and return that evening.

Willie lingered for a time. He nursed his feelings, wanting to feel justified in what he had said. He knelt down on the prie dieu in the sacristy and continued his cloudy ruminations.

At times like these he wasn't sure that he was praying. Was he simply speaking to himself and hoping God might be listening? Perhaps there was no difference in his mind between the two. Feelings of remorse began to creep into his being, sifting like some mysterious vapor through his spirit, entering the deepest part of his being. He could have sworn that some physical transformation was taking place in him. That recurring question began to rear its image. Why had he done it? Why had he taken that occasion, apparently innocent, to harangue and castigate the defenseless assistant? Even if he were right, justified, what difference did it make? Was anything gained by what he had said?

There was another part of him, however, which reached for rationalization. Wasn't it true that there was so much to be done in the parish? Meetings, the sick, convalescent homes to be visited, the grade school. When was the last time the assistant had taught an honest class to the seventh or eighth grade? Didn't those students require some instruction, some approval from a priest, as much as those in high school? Maybe more. Was Willie really wrong in what he had done? After all, it was evident that assistants these days were a different breed. They talked in terms of working at what appealed to them, special ministries that gave them the opportunity to use their special gifts. It all seemed vague and inconsequential to him. When he had been ordained he was willing to do anything that had been asked. There was so much he didn't understand about it all, too many differences to be able to take it in.

Willie heaved himself up weakly, pale with exhaustion and emotional strain. He walked toward the rectory, accompanied by those recurring doubts over whether he had really hurt the assistant. Maybe he'd talk to him and apologize when he returned. He needed a cup of coffee. Perhaps he'd rest a little and then begin his work. It was always there and he experienced a sense of frustration over its magnitude. He hadn't written any letters for several weeks because he was busy with too many other demands. He wanted to write several people who had consulted him about their problems. There was a nun who was thinking of leaving the convent because of personality differences with other members. He hadn't contacted his own sister in over a month. Perhaps he'd get to all of it today. He'd just rest a little, sit back in his chair and close his eyes.

He did work some during the day, lethargically, half-hearted about it. His depression deepened and he could feel it take hold of him physically, draining his energy and casting a gloom over his ordinarily satisfying ministry. By afternoon he was abysmally unhappy. His thinking drifted along the lines of going away for awhile, perhaps to Sante Fe and the La Fonda Hotel which he loved. He knew most of the nuns at the Loretto convent there. They treated him kindly, pampered his wants and came to him for conferences. He'd see his sister there and perhaps get some time to write letters.

In his heart he knew he probably wouldn't go. But it was pleasant to think about it, to plan ahead to a time when he could. He was better at just leaving with a moment's notice, surprising everyone, even himself, by his compulsive decisions.

Stella knew his moods and the cycle of his depressions. She always told Alice and Ruth, the secretaries. She'd say simply,

"Monsignor isn't feeling very well." It was their code, a phrase for immediate understanding, setting the three of them into a posture which called for kindness and sensitivity. Stella might cook some special dish she knew he relished.

Alice, with an extraordinary sense of humor, had known Willie since she was a young woman. Sometimes she could tease him into a better mood. There was a certain risk involved in this. Sometimes it failed and Willie refused, angrily, to be taken in. But Alice didn't mind all that much. She knew him, had an insurmountable affection for him and counted it all worth the effort. What was a little rebuff after all he had done for her?

Ruth, too, had known Willie for years. His regard and acceptance of her were essential. She had come to see him as the only priest who understood her. At times like these, when Willie was suffering, she became anxious, distraught with the need to respond. She couldn't stand to see him suffer. It brought her to tears and she took on his moods, identifying with his sense of confusion. She and Stella would whisper to each other about Willie's condition.

The assistant returned home in the late afternoon. He had the appearance of one who had worked much more than he actually had. Ordinarily a day of retreat would have been a pleasure. He usually got energy from such efforts and looked forward to them.

When he arrived, there followed those awkward greetings so familiar after scenes of friction. It was as though nothing and everything had happened; as though no one was willing to express his hurt and disappointment. Yet it was still there. The assistant was convinced that it was not his fault but, for whatever reason, felt guilty for the lack of joy in the house. Supper was a pale affair, no laughter, no attempt at cordiality, only the business of the parish. They talked about Mrs. Wytoski and how she had seemed a bit better now that she was home from the hospital. Did anyone remember to arrange for palms to be given to the shutins? There were normal overtures about willingness to take an extra mass so Willie could be freed to catch up on his work. Someone said that he had met Mr. Brandon and he seemed less irate than earlier over their failure to be present at the death of his mother. It had happened Sunday evening when no one was home.

Everyone was happy enough to end the meal and hadn't relished it or the care with which it was served. The assistant was grateful for several appointments that would keep him in the office until late. Perhaps Willie's door would be closed when he came up to his room. The other assistant, who had escaped any direct confrontation thus far, was glad to slip quietly upstairs where he turned on the television at a low volume and gave himself over to working crossword puzzles, a favorite pastime.

Night came on slowly, enveloping that great stone house that had been home for so many years. Willie came over and sat for a long time in the quiet of evening. It is the duty of a church to unobtrusively offer comfort, to insinuate itself into the thinking of those who come for a visit. I hoped Willie might console himself, thinking of what he had accomplished, how he'd been a good pastor. He sighed deeply several times and I thought I saw tears come into his eyes.

He began to pray in a round of thoughts which he offered by way of consideration on the difficulties of his life. In thinking of what had happened that day, how it had begun with a restless and sleepless night, he pondered how he might avoid such falls in time to come. It was a question he'd often asked, about which he'd prayed before. He was astute enough to know that what had happened wasn't necessarily the worst catastrophe and was not irreparable. It was just that he wished he could avoid such painful encounters in the future. But somehow he knew this wouldn't be the last time. The mysterious appearance of depression was so unpredictable, so furtive, stealing into his inner self. It seemed unfair, a travesty.

What should he do? First of all he'd have to face the assistant, and Willie wasn't good at direct apologies, especially with members of the household. He did better with parishioners, where the task was not so demeaning.

He thought of other encounters, the fractures which had mounted up in his life. There were the times he had demanded that others concede, obey because he was the pastor. Once he had confronted a nun about the way she was teaching her class, taking too much time for "creative writing" and not enough for other subjects. What did he know about teaching? He had even been acrimonious and cynical toward some of the parishioners at times, publicly accusing one of them of not knowing his job when they had a meeting about a school addition. He took umbrage at a suggestion that the contractor and architect should be hired by a board of parishioners and that the project be closely monitored by persons other than himself. He'd lost his equanimity and later suggested to the assistants that his antagonist drank too much. He knew the assistants didn't take him all that seriously at these times, but, still, he'd said it and he knew he would have been better — a better priest — had he left it unsaid.

He thought of the assistant he had harrassed just that morning. It hadn't been the first time. Perhaps there was even a detectable pattern. It seemed to him now that he had done the same thing to other assistants. He couldn't excuse them completely and returned to thoughts about how different they were these days. They took time off regularly and weren't as serious as he wanted them to be about work and application. He hadn't taken a day off in all the time he'd been a priest. He was mortally offended once when an assistant suggested that might be one of his problems and that if he got away occasionally he would be better for it. Once he confronted another assistant about going away for his weekly day off when there was work to do. The assistant too readily acquiesced, put on his cassock and sat down to work. It hadn't turned out at all the Willie wanted it to and he ended up commanding the assistant to go away for the day.

He prayed on, thinking through what had happened, wanting to change it all, wishing those depressions might leave him. One thing became certain. He would reconcile with the assistant, think of some way to ask for pardon.

Returning to his room in a quieter mood, Willie picked up a book by Cardinal Newman, his favorite author, so stentorian and clear in his thinking, and read for awhile. Actually, he was waiting for the assistant to finish downstairs. Time passed and

Willie dozed a bit in his chair. When he heard the assistant approaching, Willie called out and waited for him to appear at the open door. "I've been thinking," he began, "you're really doing most of the counseling around here, and your work at the high school is important."

Willie paused to let what he was saying take effect. It was his way of admitting quietly that he appreciated what the assistant was doing.

"I thought it might be good if you took a few days off to rest a little. It will be Holy Week soon, and you'll need all the energy you can get, what with confessions, the ceremonies and all. You do most of that, too. I know that and appreciate it. I'm grateful that you are here."

The assistant wanted to be graceful, acknowledge Willie's generosity and thank him for it. But he only nodded, afraid perhaps of his own emotions and aware that this scene was a repetition of times past. Such largess on the part of Willie hadn't really changed anything. The assistant had not yet matured to the point where he felt a sense of confidence in his abilities. He was afraid that what happened here might somehow sour and cause further tension later. He accepted gifts cautiously.

"I know you always go off a few days after Easter," Willie continued. "Don't worry about not being able to do that because you're taking time off now. We'll manage to get by. Just depend on the fact that you can have the same time you always do."

The assistant nodded again and said something to the effect he really didn't need to leave at this time. There was his obligation at the high school, and he'd scheduled several appointments. But Willie continued in a mildly persistent manner.

"Why don't you try to reschedule your appointments for next week? I'll call the principal at the high school to tell her it was my suggestion that you go away, that I felt you were tired and working too hard."

Willie gave the impression he wasn't in the mood to discuss the matter further. The assistant went to his room, confused and mystified, but sure that he had been here before. Previous similar encounters had resulted in a new television, a replacement of the worn-out carpeting in his room, a better typewriter and a recommendation that the parish might do well to install a separate telephone for him since he received so many personal calls.

It was Willie's way of mending those periodic fractures which were the bane of his life. He would send a coffee cake, a basket of fruit, flowers and candy to those whom he thought he might have offended. He sent such gifts at other times, too. He depended on them to say what he sometimes couldn't say in words, couldn't bring himself to express because it might come too close to his hidden feelings.

The assistant was grateful enough, but he felt cheated. He thought he deserved to be angry and mulish. He should have had a few days to pout, to steep in self pity. He had been offended for no reason, in his estimation. Now he had to be grateful and smile, as though nothing had happened, as though it were his fault and not Willie's. It all seemed unfair, beyond what he thought he had been called to do. Did a day or two away really make up for what had happened?

What the assistant didn't understand was that Willie was doing his best, just as much as the assistant, when he staggered under the burden of his own shortcomings. If Willie could have explained how he got into those moods, how he lost something of his better self when he said the wrong things, lashed out and became bombastic and truculent, the assistant might have been more sympathetic. But Willie couldn't. He had to deny that there was any pattern. Every time it happened, he resolved that it was the last time. What the assistant failed, further, to understand was that Willie was driven by some inner need to be everything that people expected him to be. He was gifted beyond most, but he was human and subject to the same weaknesses that others are. People just thought he ought to be more than they were. Willie knew that he wasn't, at least not to the degree that he was comfortable with their expectations.

I would be happy to end the story here by relating that Willie slept peacefully that night, with a sense of having solved all that had happened. But I know he didn't, because I saw the light blink on and off several times as the night wore on. Undoubtedly, as had happened in the past, there was only a gradual easing of those recurring pains he felt at these times. Willie could put those awkward issues behind him eventually, but not all at once. There was always a residue of anxiety lingering inside of him. He repeatedly labored over how he could have done it all differently. Eventually he managed to put the feelings aside and look optimistically to more balance and the lighter aspects of his work. He knew he wasn't perfect, regardless of what the people thought. He felt guilty at times because they insisted that he was. Sometimes he caught a flash of his inner self as an imposter, but it never lasted long and he was comforted by the conviction that he was good, that he did his best and had to accept weakness in himself as part of his makeup.

Let me finish with a few observations, if such is permissible from an old, disappeared church. It is on my mind that most people are like Willie, suffer the same kinds of cycles and recurring mysteries in their own lives. Simply put, there is in most of us a darker side which periodically appears, for reasons which remain incomprehensible and puzzling. Those who don't have to deal with such agonies are fortunate indeed. They are an exception. For the rest, there is that continuing reminder that life is never absolutely dependable, that its direction founders at times and leaves us beset with those quandaries which seldom admit to obvious solutions. I cannot tell you why this is. Could it be the moon, changes in weather, something about the cycles of the body? Whatever it is, it affects most people, some more than others, some so strongly that they have to struggle mightily with it for life.

In my years at Fourteenth and Detroit, overlooking the surrounding environs, I learned a great deal. Now it is one thing to learn and another entirely to benefit by it. One of the unforgettable truths I've learned is that reality is not always what it appears to be. An obvious truth, you say, but it's not always readily accepted. Permit me to explain.

For years, the priests who lived here came in to pray. That

included the divine office, a daily series of prayers, psalms and readings that took about an hour to complete. It was a singular opportunity for me to "join in" by looking over their shoulders and praying along with them.

A fascinating part of the recitation was what we called "The Second Nocturn." It was a reading on the life of some saint for that particular day. For example, you could have St. Theresa one day, St. Francis of Assisi another, St. Catherine of Sienna for a third and so on. The reading was meant to inspire priests with the virtue of those saints and challenge them to exemplify those same virtues, to put something of that saint's life into the priest.

What always struck me was that the saint of the day seemed so holy as to be almost inhuman, without the flaws and seams so much a part of the lives of the people I knew.

A reading about St. Francis of Assisi might relate how he never had bad thoughts and avoided them at all costs. As an illustration, the Second Nocturn related how he once passed a beautiful woman and, rather than think about her, lest he have a bad thought or two, he hurled himself dispassionately into a patch of thorn bushes. Obviously, it's almost impossible to sustain any unbecoming thoughts with all that pain and discomfort. I found myself seriously wondering if St. Francis actually did that. Is it possible that someone made that up? Such drastic reactions on the part of a saint might make the rest of us feel there is no use in even trying to be holy.

I remember other stories even more incredible. There was one about a man who lived atop a pillar for his entire adult life. People used to come by and throw what he needed up to him. The nocturn didn't say, but I presume his mother would beg him to come down because he looked so foolish up there it was giving the family a bad name. But he didn't because he knew this was what God wanted him to do, to be holy and set an example for people about what religion demanded. I know it is a little irreverent, but I used to think, when that nocturn came around, that even God might have been a little embarrassed by what that man (Simon, I think his name was) did.

There were other stories of saints who never ate anything except the bread of communion. Others never took a bath, as though such was virtuous. Still others wore chains and spiked belts under their clothing. Some never spoke to another living human being, only to God.

I suppose those who wrote about the saints wanted to do their best and exaggerated just a bit. It must have been out of love for them or at least from some desire to assure us that we should never forget them. I would not want to belittle their efforts, but I've always thought we needed a few more saints with human features, more struggle and a realistic mixture of both good and bad in their lives. For a fact, I know that some of the saints weren't all that perfect. As a church, staying in one place all those years, I've heard much the ordinary person might not know. I remember an old nun saying to Willie, here in church, that Mother Cabrini, who was later made an official saint, wasn't a very easy companion. She was temperamental and impatient with the mistakes of the other nuns, shouting at them for their apparent incompetence. Just hearing that made me feel a little better about the saints. I have nothing against Mother Cabrini. It simply offers some comfort to know that she was human.

Some people say Willie was a saint. I'm not sure anymore what the basis for becoming a saint is. I know they have an investigation to see how good a person really was, scrutinizing any negative aspects in the candidate's past that might put him or her in a bad light. A miracle or two is required, evidence of some phenomenal happenings which can be attributed to the "saint" in question. All this isn't a simple process and takes many years to complete. I'm told it also takes a good deal of money to pay all those investigators and for the grand celebration when the saint is finally canonized.

I don't think Willie was a saint. He accomplished some phenomenal objectives and contributed magnanimously to the lives of many people. For all that, he would be the first to disclaim anything remotely "second-nocturnish" about him. If he wasn't a saint, he was most times saintly, but he wasn't the type of saint you would canonize.

I want to remember Willie the way he was and not distort his genuine character. He was a blend of many human qualities. He had good days, lots of them. He was sensitive and caring. Hardly a day went by when he wasn't in tune with the parish and its members. He was present and highly visible in times of tragedy and pain. He sometimes left a meal or walked out of a ceremony so he could be with someone who might otherwise have been alone in a difficult time.

I want to remember Willie as a person with too much energy, someone who found it extremely difficult to relax and sit quietly. I wouldn't be telling the whole story, like those second nocturns, if I didn't remember his faults. He did become angry, often said the wrong thing and humiliated others because he was so sure he was right. He demanded much and couldn't always understand why the people around him didn't give it.

No, Willie wasn't a saint. I don't think he'd want to be. What would he talk about with those who lived apart, never sinned, saw life differently, mistrusted the world, and never had any distractions in prayer?

It is my rather strong conjecture that there is only one desire in Willie's life now. That is to be with all the people he ever knew, perhaps asking for another chance with some of them and promising, because he sees more clearly now, that he'd do it better next time. For all that, he did well enough the first time, enough to be remembered and loved.

Chapter Nine

THE OTHER SIDE OF THE STREET

There is much conversation these days about directions and changes in the church. We have coined words and phrases to describe the level of thinking at which people find themselves, talk about their leanings and convictions in religion. We speak of "conservatives" who would like to go back to the days when it was all simpler, more structured than it is now. Contrast these with "liberals" who are inclined to move forward, discarding what seems unworkable, thinking in terms of what is going on "out there" in the world of struggle and ferment, wanting religion to fit the needs of the people.

In my experience, a church building with a long history, there is really no such person as a total conservative or liberal. Take Willie for example. He might have celebrated mass differently from any other priest who ever came here. He would stop whenever he thought it appropriate to make a remark or two. He did that especially with children, thinking it was a select opportunity to teach. He could be described in this regard as a flaming liberal, since he disregarded sacred, long-standing prescripts about gesture, intonation, flow and continuity.

But Willie often remarked that he would leave the church if they ever changed some doctrine pertaining to the traditional teachings of the eternal faith.

I've always maintained that Willie died at the proper time. I'm not sure he could have dealt with some of the changes that have taken place since his death. It might have changed his life, embittered him and caused deep cynicism. He might have felt he had no place in the modern church.

One solid reality which Willie emphasized, a level at which

his conservatism flourished, was his attitude toward nuns. He had a rigidly specific notion of what they should represent, to him and to the parish. That notion was based on what he'd grown to appreciate and accept over a long period of time. To Willie, a Sister was dedicated to teaching, or some similar service, that took all her energy and concentration. There were other duties such as prayer, simplicity, poverty, unquestioning obedience and selfless submission. These, however, were subservient to that primary effort that was the reason for her vocation and existence.

It was a simple formula, which by today's standards might seem unrealistic. The life of the modern nun has broadened to include many missions. Some are doing things Willie would never have dreamed possible — working as pastoral assistants, liturgists, theologians of imposing prominence, teaching scripture, working as social reformers and walking at the edge of many public issues of the day.

Willie's vision of the Sisters was limited, to say the least. He saw them in flowing black habits, set off by those white borders and long rosaries hanging from their belts. They were dependably prompt, always available, never out of the house in the evening. They taught, trained, admonished, coddled the slow learner, were always patient and tolerant, offered loyalty to the faith of everyone and found their identity in "duty."

Willie loved the Sisters intensely. He made every effort to make them feel appreciated and loved, assured them that they were needed by the school and the parish. Without them, he often said, there would be no parish, no education, no need to remain in existence. He believed all this so firmly that he somehow felt that any movement away from those fundamentals would mean the loss of something essential. If a Sister questioned the meaning of her life, he found her reaction difficult. He quailed at any modernizing the Sisters undertook, even took it as personal and vindictive.

Most Sisters who came here knew about Willie long before their arrival. Stories about him circulated among them, detailing his character and sometimes enigmatic behavior. Many were happy to come because of assurance of fair treatment. Some of the younger ones recently in vows and on their first assignment, feared his forceful personality and the range of his powerful vocabulary. They saw him as a fretful, aging man who demanded obedience and respect. But they soon found that he was more benign than they had thought, a pastor in the best sense of the word. Sometimes there were unavoidable frictions. In fairness to Willie, he always tried to offer reconciliation and peace, sometimes on his own terms, but sincere and honest. Some complained that he favored one over another, a privilege traditionally awarded to pastors, it seems. I'm afraid this was true, a characteristic which Willie maintained to the end. Perhaps it was the frailty of the human structure in him.

Willie always remained firm in his demand that the first duty of the Sister was the school. Whatever they wanted in that regard, he readily gave. Pupils were to be awarded the best education possible in the eight years given to them. Willie looked upon that time as the cradle of faith, the source of future priests and Sisters, deeply Christian mothers and fathers, the devoted Catholic lay person. No cost, no effort, was too great.

There were, of course, other duties, but all secondary to the obligation of teaching. There were PTA meetings, conferences, recitals and plays. There were Sunday classes for those unfortunate victims of public education, the lesser standard of the day. The Sisters taught the boys to serve at mass, undertook Confirmation preparation, occasionally took classes themselves at local colleges and sometimes visited the sick. First, however, was that time-honored service of identity with the Catholic school.

It is true that those roles apart from teaching frequently offered release from tension and anxiety. Take the training of servers, for example. Hardly a Sister who came here wasn't chosen to train altar boys. Willie prided himself on having well trained servers and carefully selected those Sisters who, he thought, had a particular ability along these lines.

No Sister began by training boys to serve at mass. This prestigious position was offered only to those who had proved themselves in lower ranks, worked up through benediction, stations of the cross and Saturday night novenas. The zenith was reserved to those who trained servers for funerals. That level was the end of the continuum. There was nothing higher.

I remember when Sister Thomasine came to teach. She was young, perhaps on her first assignment. Willie immediately assigned her to training servers for benediction. This wasn't the most coveted job a Sister could have and was, as a matter of fact, solicitously avoided by most. Sister Thomasine, being young and at the lower end of the order of importance in the convent, naturally fell in line for the task. It didn't seem particulary difficult, though, and she thought she could do it with about a half-hour for each candidate. After all, benediction wasn't that complex. The priest simply came out, flanked by the servers who assisted him at several simple tasks. There were two incensings, both at obvious and easily remembered times. The last was followed by a chant at the end of which a silk cope, the humeral veil, was placed over the priest's shoulders for a blessing with the monstrance. Certainly nothing too difficult about that.

Sister Thomasine had heard stories about accidents and clumsy antics by some of the servers. They were laughable and hardly related to the task at hand. Once someone had turned the thurible upside down and dropped the live coals on the sanctuary carpet. Another time one of the boys was seized with a spasm of coughing from the smoke of the burning incense which caused him to throw up. Someone told a tale, obviously exaggerated, about a careless server who simply threw the remaining live coals in the waste basket after benediction. They smoldered for half the night and finally burst into flame. It was later determined that, except for a stroke of fortune, perhaps a miracle, the church could have burned down.

Sister Thomasine was determined that none of this would eventuate while she was in charge of benediction. She set out methodically to train the servers, meticulously taking pains to instruct them on how to hold the thurible upright, not to breathe in the smoke and where to dispose of the live coals afterward. Actually, it was quite simple if one went about it properly;

approached the job with interest, encouraged the servers and offered personal support.

The evening of the first benediction came. It was an added demand of Willie that the Sister in charge of training should attend the ceremony, something about being on hand to observe and offer further suggestions. Sister Thomasine faithfully complied, wanting to be there anyway to see her students do their best work and impress Willie with their precision and demeanor.

They did just that. Everything went extremely well with proper genuflections, bows, hands neatly folded, posture erect and dignified. The servers didn't miss a cue and actually anticipated Willie's every move, held the thurible upright at the proper level and stood patiently at his side as he ladled the grains of incense onto the glowing coals. Willie loved incense and gloried in swinging the thurible up in wide arcs which left thick trails of blue smoke filling the sanctuary and filtering into the body of the church. The boys took it all in style and gave the confident impression that they'd done it all before. They knew Sister Thomasine was in the front pew observing them, but didn't dare glance her way. It was going very well.

The second incensing was finished and the ceremony reached that moment of high solemnity just before the benediction. Willie intoned the ancient versicle of hallowed praise: "Panem de celo praestitisti eis," to which Iva, the choir of one, obediently sang in reply: "Omne delectamentum in se habentem."

There followed then a sung prayer which was to signal the server on the right that he was to walk over to the edge of the sanctuary, take up the humeral veil and place it reverently on Willie's shoulders at the end of the chant. But the server didn't move, perhaps mesmerized by what he was doing, thinking of Sister Thomasine's praise and his parents' delight and approval.

Beads of moisture began to appear on Sister Thomasine's forehead and upper lip. She concentrated intensely. Perhaps she whispered just audibly, "Philip, for heaven's sake, get the humeral veil." But Philip was lost in a trance, an ecstasy of euphoria, intoxicated by the wine of this new and holy experience.

Several times during the sung prayer Willie looked ominously at Philip, but to no avail. Everything was finished and there followed a sinister silence. Still Philip did not move. It was as though he had ascended to a level of contemplation wholly beyond young boys, a communion with what is entirely sanctified.

Willie turned and looked directly at Sister Thomasine. She could only gaze respectfully toward the altar without any idea of what to do. She wanted to shout at Philip, "Go get the humeral veil." She thought Willie might say something to Philip. Nothing.

Finally, Willie began to gesture boldly by tapping the tops of his shoulders with his hands. Philip roused himself from reverie and hurried over to the table, took up the humeral veil and placed it over his own shoulders, then knelt down quickly and resumed his meditation.

By now everyone was aware that pandemonium had struck the sanctuary and who could tell where it might lead. The one significant exception was Sister Thomasine, who had retreated into her own reverie. She could never say for sure how that benediction ended. She could only recall that it was eventually finished and she decided to exit by the side door rather than to walk to the back and all those people.

You might think that this debut was the end of her career, but it was not. Willie saw her good will and in time she rose to the highest level of training servers for funerals. That went quite well for her and, aside from a few minor problems such as someone spilling the holy water or stepping on Willie's cope, she rose to grace and acceptance. She kept her job for many years, hoping to pass it on to some unsuspecting successor, but never having the appropriate opportunity to do so.

Where is Philip today? I wonder. I hope he is succeeding and finding satisfaction in his pursuits, whatever they are. I suspect he is less organized and astute than some, but a person of good will. Perhaps he has maintained that early penchant for reveries. In my estimation, we need his kind of person who has that aplomb and good nature that make us smile. It is my educated guess that, wherever he is, he remembers his days as a server with joy and considers it a vital part of his history.

As I said, Willie loved the Sisters. He tried always to make their stay pleasant and worthwhile and regretted their departure when they were transferred. He often offered them counsel and hoped they would accept him as one who supported and encouraged them.

Not only Willie loved the Sisters. They were revered and cherished by every parishioner. Parents readily relinquished the care and destiny of beloved children into their hands, trusting that the outcome would be far better than anything of which parents were capable. Every Sister took that trust deeply, seriously, and offered her best in behalf of those who came under her charge.

Had we been able to recognize it, perhaps we could have admitted that the Sisters were among the first to offer a deeper sensitivity to those who were neglected in the history of the Church. There was something about them, maybe their gifts as women, their willingness to share the sufferings and needs of those who had been missed by the message of the gospel. People felt good around them, as though something of their life could rub off to penetrate the harder core of those who were "outside" the pale of deeper sensibilities. Many found themselves inclined to follow those gifts of spirit which pertained more particularly to their way of life. Children and adults trusted them, perceived something completely genuine in them which offered comfort and acceptance.

I remember one Sunday after 9:30 mass when Judge Horan, a dignified, longtime parishioner, rang the bell at the rectory. When one of the assistants answered, the judge stood serenely at the door with a five year old child clutching his hand. "I found this boy walking alone down Fourteenth Avenue, Father. I've asked his name, but I think he might be too frightened to talk to me. I suspect he might have been at mass, being dressed the way he is and all alone. I wonder if he didn't get separated from his family somehow?"

The assistant, somewhat skeptical, didn't see how a child of five could have gotten lost from his family, but felt certain that with a little tact and persuasion he could obtain whatever information necessary to clear up the situation. After all, the judge was a tall and imposing gentleman, better suited for courts and handing down wise decisions. Obviously he was a little threatening to the boy.

The priest knelt down to the level of the boy, leaning toward him affably in an acceptably psychological procedure, he thought, to reduce fear. In his gentlest tone he inquired, "Can you tell us what your name is?" Nothing. The priest persisted, assuming a slightly different direction of inquiry. Maybe the problem was that the boy didn't know his own name. At what age do children identify, when do they know who they are? He asked another question. "Where do you go to school?" If they could learn what school he attended, they might be able to ask further questions about his teacher, ingratiate themselves, win his confidence and go on to solve the problem of what to do with him.

Still nothing. Further attempts were equally futile and the priest was beginning to lose his composure. Maybe he ought to get a little stern and insist that the obviously spoiled and perhaps disobedient child confess or else. He didn't have all day and had to start thinking about the eleven o'clock mass. But the boy would have none of it and remained firmly mute.

Suddenly the priest thought of the Sisters. He disliked admitting failure, but perhaps they might know him and, if not, at least know how to handle the situation. They dealt with children every day.

The priest suggested to the judge that they take the boy over to the convent. They went out the back door in procession, the priest leading and the judge coming close behind with the boy still clutching his hand. They rang the convent bell and waited hopefully for the appearance of a familiar face. The priest looked disdainfully at the boy once again, miffed by his silence and refusal to cooperate in such a simple matter. He was about to open the subject of his name again when the door opened. Sister Marie Joann smiled at the gathered party and offered a cheerful morning greeting. Immediately the boy disentangled himself from the judge and leaped into the arms of his kindergarten teacher. His tongue completely loosed now, he explained to Sister that he was lost, catching his breath in sobs, explaining further that his family left him at the church door and he didn't know where they were. Would she help him find them, please, and he promised to be good forever.

Sister Marie Joann caressed and calmed him, explaining to the mystified judge and priest that it was Fred Diss, her student. The judge offered some audible assent, what might have been discerned as typical court room procedure, and the priest protested that if he'd just been able to get the child to talk there would have been no problem.

After a few additional remarks, Fred's father drove up to the church, solving the unraveling mystery. With nine children, it was easy enough to miss one of them in the aftermath of a hectic Sunday crowd. It wasn't until the family had arrived at a restaurant and ordered breakfast that someone asked where Fred might be and it was discovered that he was missing. With that, his father had hurriedly returned to the church. Fred was found, not in the temple speaking to learned men, but in the arms of his teacher, Sister Marie Joann.

Isn't life that way? You would expect the priest would certainly be able to solve just about every problem which might arise in any parish, especially with the able assistance of a wise judge. It is true: the weak things of the world God has chosen to confound the strong, and the foolish to overcome the wise. Imagine, a five year old causing that much consternation in a seasoned judge and an educated priest! And a Sister, the youngest in the community at that time, being so significant and protective!

It has occurred to me over the years that the Sisters were always revered and accepted by just about everyone in the parish. They were a willing group, ready to help and support a great variety of projects and individuals who were in need. I remember them at their best, doing what parents sometimes neglected, teaching children about God, giving catechism classes, engendering lifelong devotion to faith and the meaning of existence. I was always amazed at how they did all they were asked, smiled through it and had still more energy for other things. What is more fascinating, they were apparently happy, laughed a lot — more, I have to confess, than most of the priests I've known. They seemed to get more of that happiness which comes from serving others, the reason why they embraced their way of life in the beginning.

I admired that lighter side. One of the stories Willie loved and repeated often was about an incident which took place in the kindergarten when Sister Rosemary was teaching. It was her method to relate a little story from the Gospels every day, describe something from the life of Jesus. She'd parcel it out in colorful detail and language understandable to those innocent minds. She took her time and let what she was saying create its own picture in their imaginations. She wanted them to remember, because she would ask them the next day to repeat the story. When one of them did, she gave some kind of reward for their effort, a bookmark or perhaps a piece of candy.

On one occasion Sister Rosemary told about the marriage feast at Cana where Jesus had changed water into wine, saving the day and helping the hosts of the occasion avoid embarrassment at their lack of foresight. When she asked the next day who remembered the story, Paul, a bright and uninhibited child, raised his hand and courageously began to recount the episode. "Jesus and Mary were at a big party," he related confidently, his eyes shining. Gaining momentum with the sound of his own voice, he turned more fully toward the rest of the class and continued with something of a flourish. "But they ran out of beer. And Mary said to Jesus, 'They don't got no more beer.'"

Such an accounting was satisfying enough for the attentive listeners and everyone, save their teacher, was content with the accuracy of Paul's rendition. Wondering what the outcome to such an apparently insoluble dilemma might be, the children craned closer to hear what Jesus might do, as though they had never heard the story before. Paul told them that Jesus simply said, "Let them drink water."

Sister Rosemary could hardly withold the promised reward because of a few discrepancies. The essence of the story was certainly there; someone was in trouble and Jesus helped. What more could be added?

On another occasion Sister told them about how, after the Resurrection, Jesus appeared to Mary Magdalene. She thought he was the gardener and was amazed when Jesus said, "Mary," indicating who he was and that he recognized her. Mary Magdalene naturally wanted to touch him to make sure he was real. But Jesus declined, saying, "Don't touch me. I am going to God." Recognizing that this was not the total passage, Sister Rosemary wanted them at least to gain the notion that Jesus was returning to heaven, a difficult concept for children of five. The children, as always, listened with fervor, as though they understood perfectly, eyes bright, offering maximum concentration.

The next day, eager to test their retention, she asked who could recite the previous day's lesson. One of the girls this time asked to respond.

The story began well enough, details in order and sequence at least similar. Jesus was in the garden, that was clear. The name of Mary Magdalene had been forgotten, understandably enough, and was reverently referred to as "This Lady." When "This Lady" saw Jesus she wanted to "put her arms around him." Sister Rosemary had never thought of it, but agreed that this rendition might be a better translation than the original.

The child continued. "This Lady saw Jesus and wanted to put her arms around him. Then Jesus said to the lady, 'Don't touch me, Mary, I got a brand new body.'"

The trouble with humor in kindergarten classes is that no one laughs except the teacher. The students took it all in with perfect equanimity, credulous to the highest degree, unquestioning and properly sober. There wasn't a smile among them. After all, that's exactly how the story went, wasn't it? Details and incidentals were meaningless to them. The outcome from what was said the day before as compared to today was exactly the same. Sister Rosemary could only smile. Later she would relate the story to her companions. It was worth waiting to tell. It would enrich not only her own life but that of many to come. Children! How often we think we are giving when, instead, we lavishly receive.

No wonder Willie loved the Sisters. They were lifeblood to so many people, so much of what is important to everyone. I have the impression, admittedly a figment of my imagination, that when individuals die they are welcomed to heaven by everyone who preceded them in death. I see this long, double row of smiling people forming a kind of corridor through which that person walks, shaking hands and receiving the loving gratitude of all. I think that corridor is longest of all when nuns enter after death. They were here, present in countless ways, as long as I can recollect. Wherever they are now, out there, teaching still, in even broader and more effective modes, I want them to know I remember.

Chapter Ten

A DAY IN THE LIFE OF MARIGOLD

She must have walked past the rectory several times. It was early morning, just after four. She hadn't been near a church for a long time. She couldn't remember exactly. There were those images of former days, the swishing black habits of grade school nuns and the priest who came occasionally to teach catechism, but otherwise preached at a distance on Sunday. Sometimes she thought of these things before going to sleep. Lately, she found, they depressed her, swept her with a lingering melancholy that became difficult to shrug off.

She was twenty-four, she explained, born and raised in a small town. The priest forgot just where. She only mentioned it once, so it was reasonable he would forget that insignificant detail of her life. She had come to speak of much more important issues.

Marigold, a courageous woman, had experienced more of life at twenty-four than many individuals twice her age. When she began to think about what she was doing now, though, she speculated that this had taken more courage than anything she had ever done before. She wasn't sure why she came but was conscious of some force that had led her here.

She told herself she'd give them thirty seconds, ring once more, wait another thirty and, if no one came, she would give up. She kept trying to figure out why she'd come. She had been drinking some, not as much as other nights, though. She was certainly "in control." She waited, half hoping no one would answer.

She was just turning to leave when a light flashed on inside. The door opened and she found herself facing the priest.

She wanted to turn and run, not because the priest frightened her, looked angry or said anything negative. He was too sleepy for such reactions. She wanted to run because it had cost her a lot of energy and time to "leave" those old religious feelings and that heavy sense of oppression connected, somehow, with religion. God knows she didn't have to go back to those days, to her parents, to all that preaching and anxiety, to the warning that God was so easily angered and waited for her to sin so he could punish her, banish her from the path of grace. What was she doing here? Maybe she'd say something simple — ask what time morning mass was or request directions to the bus stop.

The priest, who stood those few seconds while all those thoughts passed before her, asked, not unkindly, "Would you like to come in?" She had hoped he might be a little curt, even truculent. It would have been easier to leave. As though he were reading her mind, he smiled a little. Was it genuine? Was he laughing at her?

She didn't say anything and simply stepped inside when he opened the door. They went into a small office together and he asked her, politely, to sit down.

She thought he might open the conversation by commenting on something or other, even offering some reassurance that it was all right for her to be there. But he only sat. He didn't say anything. He smiled again and waited. Perhaps he was thinking about the sleep he was missing, what he had to do that day.

Finally he said, gently, "How can I help you?" It was then she began to cry, tentatively at first, a few tears, a tremor and almost inaudible sob. Then she dropped her head and her body shook with what appeared to be the finality of long anticipation, the end of patient waiting. She forgot his presence, or at least put it aside for the moment. He sat, not looking at her, not wanting to intrude. It seemed private to him, her time alone. He waited.

He was not at first struck by her beauty. She seemed only a shadow in the doorway, standing a little aside. As she sat there, bent in sadness, he began to look more closely at her and was fascinated by the lines of her face, her slender body. She was well dressed, neat and appealing. A faint aroma of redolent perfume evoked in him a distinct response of pleasure and warmth. He found himself somewhat preoccupied with her and thought immediately of celibacy, the priesthood, his vows. He was young and had not yet fathomed the depth of those feelings within him.

She began now to breathe more deeply, struggling to maintain a semblance of calm. Finally she began to speak. It had been years since she had been in a church. She had never visited a priest, never spoken to one, outside of confession and those desultory remarks offered in greetings at church. She was Catholic, of course, had been all her life. She paused and looked directly into the priest's eyes. "I thought I'd given religion up, but lately it seems to be coming back to haunt me. All those old thoughts about God and the Church sometimes crowd in on me, when I least expect them. I thought if I talked to a priest I might get some help. I don't want to go back. I don't know what I want to do."

The priest listened and said that he wanted to help in any way he could. She responded obliquely, as though speaking to herself. "I've been out all night, walking, trying to think."

Life had gone well enough for her. She had moved to Denver in hopes of getting a job, an apartment, and finding satisfaction in the city. It hadn't been easy. Her mother and father were opposed and told her she should stay home. There was plenty to do there, with her own kind, her friends from way back. What could she find in the city that wasn't right there?

"I couldn't make them understand," she continued. "I wanted more. I couldn't stand the thought of becoming like my mother and my older sisters — married, having children, never going anywhere. When I looked at them and saw how old they were getting, doing the same thing everyday, I knew I had to leave."

"I'm glad I left. Everybody there knows everything about everyone else. If you do something in the morning, it's all over the place by evening. It's not my idea of life." She ended with emphasis.

The priest nodded, listening and in no hurry to contribute, giving the impression that he understood and could see why she had made her decision to leave that small community.

She went on, perhaps because the priest made no sign that he wanted to say anything just then. "The church was just like everything else in town. Priests seem to stay there forever. They are mostly older and preach the same sermons every Sunday, year after year, about how to be a better Catholic, how God expects it. Women are expected to stay at home, have families, wait on the men."

Some hidden vigor took over as she spoke and her voice grew more intense. "Sometimes they talked about purity, the virtue most expected of Catholic girls. They told us to be cautious and never compromise ourselves. Another regular subject was birth control and how God provides for children and blesses parents who obey the teaching of the Church."

She said it was all too much.

So she left one morning. She took the bus to Denver. She remembered it vividly and could still recall the scene in detail. Her mother wept and her father looked on silently, angry and hurt. She hadn't felt much as she said goodbye — a kind of sadness for her mother, a sense of resentment toward her father who would not speak to her. Her only distinct recollection was that it was a long ride.

She had gotten mostly small jobs since arriving about a year ago. She had been a waitress for awhile and that had turned into an opportunity to work in a cocktail lounge. It meant a little more money and a chance to meet people. She hadn't always met "ideal" men, the kind the priests in her home town had talked about — Catholic, dependable, strong, like the saints and early Christian heroes. The men she met these days were at least interesting, and knew how to talk about something besides the little subjects of small towns. Sometimes she went out with men, hoping she didn't appear crude or show her small town background. Most of these were men she met at the lounge, which meant going out after two or three in the morning.

She had to admit they weren't the kind of men she would have preferred and knew they sometimes took her out because they hoped she would go to bed with them. But she liked their polite manners and didn't go out with them a second time if they treated her badly. She knew she was appealing enough to be discriminating. She hoped, eventually, to meet the "right guy" and have a steady boyfriend.

It seemed natural, at least logical, that she would be going to bed with them. It wasn't something she had planned, but she liked the affection and closeness. She knew a few women, too, and occasionally went to a movie or dinner with them. But it wasn't the same, not like it was when she was with men. She reminded herself that she shouldn't be doing what she was doing, and resolved from time to time to reform. Still, it didn't seem that bad. It was a different world and she liked it. People she met at the lounge seemed happy, without the cares she had left in that small town so long before. Was it only a year ago?

Sometimes the men who came home with her gave her money as they were leaving. Sometimes they gave her presents. She never asked for anything, didn't expect it. But she didn't refuse it, either.

"Does that mean I'm a prostitute? How does that happen?" She began to cry again, silently, gripping her fingers as though they were in pain.

The priest felt a genuine sense of compassion and was grateful she had come. He was particularly thankful he hadn't reacted angrily at four in the morning. He spoke of alternatives, how he wanted to help her, how there must be people she could meet, some new directions she could take to change her life. Could she get a different job?

"I don't know. I don't want to take less pay. I have a nice apartment and I'm used to being comfortable. I don't want to go back to that life I left behind."

She changed the course of the conversation, wanting to ask him some questions. "What about my religion? If I died today, would I go to hell?"

She surprised herself speaking this way. Did she really believe in those things?

The priest talked of her goodness, how she must have wanted to change her life or she wouldn't have come. He said that a judgment of that kind was not his to make. God understands people better than priests do. It seemed so pale and shallow that he stopped in the middle of a sentence. He felt an enormous sense of inadequacy. He wondered what Jesus might have said. He remembered the woman caught in adultery and how Jesus had told her to sin no more. He was afraid to say "Sin no more" because he knew she might, might sin that night, and he didn't want her to go away with a sense of rejection. He tried to think, strained to find something that might comfort her.

As they talked, the priest felt a closeness to her. He sensed (perhaps it was his imagination) that she felt more at ease and was attracted to his gentle nature and calm reassurance.

Morning came and the room gradually filled with daylight, reminding the priest that it was First Friday. He thought of six-thirty mass and visits he would make to give communion to the sick and old. He didn't want to leave, didn't want to let her go without somehow resolving the problem. Time passed and he found himself resenting having to say mass, resenting the people who were even now beginning to gather in the church, the older ladies and school children, all in the state of grace, all close to God. He was ashamed of his thoughts and wondered what they would say if they knew he'd prefer to stay with this young woman than say mass on First Friday, a time of devotion and faith.

Finally he told her he had to go. It was after six and he hadn't shaved. He always shaved before mass. He'd never thought of it before, but it struck him as odd and made him want to go over to the church just this one morning looking exactly the way he did now, unkempt, hastily dressed.

"I have to go, too," she returned, perhaps to give the impression that she was independent of him. She regarded him steadily, unafraid.

He asked her if she could return. He would be back by nine at the latest. Could she come back? They could talk more then. Even as he said it, he knew he had to be at the high school by eleven to teach a class he hadn't yet prepared. He didn't care. He found himself resenting the high school the way he had resented the six-thirty mass and the ladies who were, by now, sitting in church.

He asked her again if she would return. "I'm sure we can come to some kind of solution." His voice gave the distinct impression of confidence, even though he wasn't sure he'd have anything new to say when she returned.

She looked at him a bit distantly. She asked him how old he was. Twenty-seven. She was twenty-four. The conversation trailed to nothing and she stood to leave. He didn't want to ask her again to return, afraid that he would overdo it and she might be offended by his insistence. She said, "Nine?" He responded, "nine." She said she would be back.

As she passed him at the door he thought he saw tears in her eyes again. She turned and it seemed her eyes were very soft, pleading for something he hoped desperately he could give her. She touched his hand gently, reminding him of his teachers in the seminary who had said he should never let anyone, especially a woman, touch him. Her hand lingered for a moment as she looked at him and said again, "Nine." Then she left.

He thought he loved her at that moment. He hoped it was the same kind of love Jesus had when he spoke to women — to the woman caught in adultery, to the prostitute from Magdala. But he wasn't sure. He felt the resentment about mass and high school slip easily away as he ran upstairs to shave. He'd skip the shower and other amenities this morning.

He said mass with attention, praying fervently in gratitude for the opportunity of seeing his work clearly, of being part of some greater plan which extended itself to sinners and those who suffered the severity of life's confusions. He gave communion to those who came to the rail, distracted only a little by thoughts about the state of grace, so easily presumed by most of the parishioners, by himself. He didn't understand much of what he'd been taught and felt he had learned vastly more since ordination than during the eight years he had spent in the seminary.

After mass he hurriedly filled the pyx with hosts and set out on his customary First Friday journey: to the convalescent home, filled with those ancient, sometimes vacant people who were in the state of grace by nature and absolute right; then to Mr. Glasser, who once protested he couldn't receive communion because he forgot that morning and smoked his pipe; then to a number of other residents scattered throughout the parish, including Mrs. Shields who always greeted him warmly and asked him to stay for breakfast, to which he always responded that he'd like to but had more communion calls. Back in his car and on to other homes, visiting the sick, greeting husbands and wives, their children, whose faces often manifested their pain. It is among life's greatest difficulties, he thought, to live with someone who is chronically ill. It is almost the same as being ill oneself, being part of someone's suffering and pain day after day. He felt the fortune of his life, the privilege of returning to the comfort of the rectory for breakfast and of being able to leave the dishes right there on the table. He thought of the luxury of it all, the second cup of coffee, the pleasant surroundings. He felt a twinge of guilt that he wasn't taking care of a sick person, that he wasn't sick himself. Did God want that of him?

He thought of Marigold. Was that really her name? He'd never heard of such a name for a woman. He hoped she would be back at nine and wondered why he thought it so important to see her again. He had a vivid image of her face, the tears in her eyes, her poignant, pleading gaze.

He pulled into the parking space reserved at the rectory, his name in black letters on the cement block. It was a little after eight-thirty. Plenty of time for breakfast. He knew Stella wouldn't have it ready. It was against her principles to start anything before she actually beheld the physical presence of anyone coming in for the morning meal. She'd left too many cold meals on the table. But she was efficient enough and would have it all there before long. On this morning, the priest wanted to be finished before nine. He didn't want Marigold waiting in his office.

He left the table with time to spare, ran upstairs to get his books ready for class, in case he had no time after she came. He was downstairs at nine and waited, ready, thinking of what he could do or say. He had what he thought were several rather effective suggestions.

She didn't come. By nine-fifteen he began to feel apprehensive. By nine-thirty he was wondering what he had said to offend her, but he knew it couldn't be that. She must have thought it over and decided not to come. Perhaps she was even afraid to return. By ten he was making a desultory effort to prepare his class.

She didn't come that day, nor the next. She never came again and he never saw her again. At first the image of her face was quite clear. He could remember the tone of her voice, its inflection of anxiety and the hint of pain. Gradually it all began to fade, taking on an indistinct character and melding eventually into that universal face which is just there, in the mind, covering all who knock at doors or come unbidden into one's life for assistance. He had to relegate her to that group he stored in those recesses. Unfinished ministry, people who came, left and never came again, never asked for help a second time. He didn't understand why and was hard on himself, thinking someone else might have been more effective. It wasn't to the point of desperation, of giving up, but it needled him and left him dispirited, wanting an explanation.

Because Marigold didn't come back, he was forced to think of the others. There was Harvard Brophy who had embezzled a large sum from a local bank. It was an incredible scandal in the parish. Brophy had been a leading parishioner, loved by everyone. He was a coach and president of the men's club. Harvard went to jail, served his time, came back and got into more trouble. As time passed, no one knew exactly where Harvard was. Was he out of jail now? There were rumors that he was wanted by the police again. Once a detective came to the rectory asking if anyone had seen him and where did the priests think he might be?

He hadn't thought of Harvard for six or seven months when, one evening after dinner he went over to the church to sit and pray. He knelt in the back and was just beginning to relax when he heard someone say, "Hello, Father."

He didn't recognize him at first. The man needed a shave, his clothes were rumpled, and he appeared to have been without a bath or sleep for some time. The priest, remembering how well groomed Harvard used to be and his handsome face and smooth hands, said, "Is that you, Harvard?" It was. They talked a little. The priest didn't ask many questions, afraid to bring up embarrassing circumstances. After a time Harvard asked to go to confession and there followed that ritual always made more sacred by the drama of sin and the pain of life.

When they finished, the priest asked Harvard what he planned to do. The once clever, dynamic, admired member of the parish could only offer some generalities, evading any definite answer. The priest asked if there might be some way he could help. He assured him that he came most nights to the church after dinner. He'd be glad to meet him any time. He said he knew that Harvard was wanted by the police and couldn't they talk about it? Harvard was welcome to call and say when he was coming. They could meet in the church. He tentatively suggested that they could talk right then and there, but Harvard said something about having an appointment to keep. He might call the priest, or maybe he'd come by the church again. But he didn't. The priest went faithfully to the church each evening, hoping Harvard might come, waiting for the voice from the corner, the way it had happened before. But he didn't come. He never came again. The priest later heard some vague story about how he had died in California, alone, without friends or family.

Another time a native Indian from South Dakota came with her daughter, who turned out to be her son. He was a transvestite who "married" a sailor in order to receive a government allotment. They had been coming regularly for money, always with the assurance that they were returning to South Dakota, or had just come from there because there was no work and if they could just have a little money they could get on with their lives. There was a job waiting, but they needed something to tide them over until they could get paid.

They were so pathetic. Perhaps they lied so smoothly because so many had lied to them and their people, telling them that they would always have a home in their native land and America would take care of them.

He wanted to help them settle down to some sort of life that might keep them from lying, stop them from moving aimlessly from one place to another. But he never could. He could only give them more money and refer them to an employment agency or to Catholic Charities. They promised, but eventually, perhaps afraid he might make them do something they didn't want to do, they stopped coming.

There was a homosexual who had periodically spoken to him of his anguish and despair over the certitude that he was lost. He implored the priest for help, for some assurance that God understood. The priest found himself so limited, so unable to contact the pain that was inside this young man, to expunge it. There were platitudes to offer, exhortations, the promise of understanding even when he knew he didn't understand.

There were mothers whose children had married outside the Church and could he do anything for them? There were couples whose child was retarded or handicapped. There were penitents who had committed the same sin, week after week, and came shamefully for absolution. He told them they were good, that they were doing what they could, were morally sound in their resolve. He often had the impression they didn't believe him and thought he must be committing the same sins they were.

There were people who practiced birth control after five or six children and could he give them permission to receive the sacraments? There were wives and husbands who were unfaithful, who wanted something more than their marriages offered, caught in depression and despair at the banality of their listless existence.

The priest listened, spoke his persuasive best, assured them of understanding, sometimes chided them for their naivete, but asked them to come back. A few did, many did not. They were still out there, somewhere, with Marigold and Harvard and the rest. He used to fantasize that they would be together in heaven — the many people whose questions had never been answered, whose lives had always remained unsettled.

The priest came often to the quiet of my sanctuary for refuge and escape. I listened to him and in my own way tried to make him think of what he had done and the good he had accomplished. A church made of mute bricks and lumber is limited in its ability to communicate. Sometimes I thought I made him feel better, more confident. He smiled about some things and thought of happier situations such as giving retreats and teaching the young and eager students at the high school.

He used to say there were really two parishes. One seemed so tranquil, composed of those who came regularly to Sunday mass, many during the week. Like his own, their lives were blessed. They came from good backgrounds, peaceful circumstances. It wasn't that there was absolute security in their lives or peace without a struggle. They suffered normal hurts and pains. They needed their faith, their community. They were good, sincere, well meaning. They were concerned for the needs of others and would do anything if asked. As in his life, stress and sadness visited them on occasion, exacted its price and demanded its toll. But there were the cushions of close family members, friends, deep faith, confidence in God's presence to support them.

The second parish was filled and overflowing, forming an endless line of those who came in pain, confusion and anger with life's insoluble problems. They were the Marigolds and Harvards who filled the city, who came, often anonymously, demanding and pleading for something more than Sunday mass, the sacraments, the Altar and Rosary Society. They were sometimes arrogant and offensive, justly so because their lives were too full of what everyone wants to avoid. Other times they came humbly and quietly to weep in the corner of the office, as though it energized and enriched them to carry on a little more, just to the top of whatever current hill or precipice confronted them.

Ministry to those in the first parish, those in the pews and generously present at gatherings and meetings, was simple, a joy. Ministry to the second was a constant challenge that called for more than he often had and he frequently had to admit defeat.

He gave as much as he knew how to give, but even in the giving was aware of how little it was. Sometimes he experienced great joy, knew that he was at the heart of the gospel, and found something similar to the very message preached in those sacred pages. Yet, when the Marigolds and Harvards came, it left him with a deep sense of need.

Then he would come over, take his turn at weeping in the corner, unobtrusively, quietly. Did it give him energy? Enrich him? I think so, because sometimes I thought he left with a lighter step and an appearance of renewed resolution.

Evening came that Friday and he went downstairs to the conference room at seven-thirty to teach the instruction class. It was designed to encourage those interested in the Catholic Church to consider and accept whatever persuasion necessary to be converted, to enter the narrow gate. He began with his usual method of introducing the subject at hand and assuring the participants of a chance for discussion. It struck him that he saw Marigold there, sitting among those people. Her image was vivid, flushed with a sense of urgency, but at home and wanting to laugh. It came to him that during those early morning hours she had not once smiled.

He wished she had come back. He wondered if about now she was beginning her work, waiting tables in the lounge. He reminded himself that the members of the class were like her — seeking, discovering, thirsty to know about God. He smiled a little at himself, at the thought of teaching it for her, wanting to give them what she hadn't gotten, a better God who understands and takes us as we are, forgiving and much larger than we can possibly conceive.

When he went to bed he was tired. The day had begun at four. It seemed such a short while ago, but he knew that much separated him from the events of that morning, infinitely more than one measured by the passing of minutes and hours. His eyes closed and he waited for eternity to come, to touch something of its magnitude in blessed sleep. In another time he would understand more clearly. He breathed deeply, gathering within himself a sense of hope.

Chapter Eleven

ALL IN A NIGHT'S WORK

If a priest can preach a good sermon, he makes up for a multitude of deficiencies in many other areas. Preaching is a traditional and long-enshrined hallmark of ministry. It might just be that there is greater demand today than ever for a well-prepared homily.

There never was any doubt that Willie could give a good sermon. He had all those unusual qualities which blend to produce the best of preachers: a resonant, well-modulated voice; graceful gestures and poised body movement; an excellent vocabulary; and a style of delivery somewhere between a persuasive evangelist and a Shakespearian dramatist.

Time was not important to him. When he got seriously into the subject he might easily go on for a half-hour. If his approach left people a little miffed at times, he compensated amply with content and substance. No one slept when Willie preached and most people went away with something positive, points for discussion and thought.

Willie knew he had that rare gift possessed by effective preachers and tried to be modest about it. Like all good orators, though, he was pleased to hear people approve and offer a remark or two of encouragement and congratulations after a particularly compelling sermon. If no one said anything on the way out of church, he'd begin to feel puzzled, a little insecure. When an appreciable amount of anxiety had built up, Willie, like all preachers (even the poorer ones), looked for some acceptable way to elicit a favorable comment. True, it wasn't nearly as pleasing to hear about it that way, but it was something he needed for assurance and motivation. He made remarks such as, "Well, I hope that was clear enough this morning." Or, he might be even a little more subtle by suggesting, "I guess I got a bit carried away."

Most times parishioners responded favorably with positive comments. "That was truly fine, Monsignor," they might say, or, "You ought to give more sermons like that one." Another might say, "I don't know how you do it, Sunday after Sunday, coming up with all those ideas."

This was high praise and offered Willie, as it would any preacher, a euphoria which could last for an entire day. It sent him back to his desk to prepare even more, reading and hoping to be current in theological trends.

With that kind of approval, which seemed always to be present, Willie felt assured about his efforts. Sometimes he reminisced about great preachers of the past — priests and missionaries who visited to give sermons at parishes for a week or ten days at a time. He liked to recall that in those days before the world became seduced by television and radio, when people didn't have so many places to go in the evening, they literally flocked to hear these powerful orators. He modestly admitted that he'd never be like any of them. He saw himself at the periphery of their circle, having some of their characteristics, sharing something, in some smaller way, of their greatness. On occasion, when all was going well, when the right words were flowing spontaneously and easily, when he knew the people were listening intently and when one could hear a pin drop, he could mildly deceive himself that he was as stentorian and effective as anyone. It was a small immodesty, a pecadillo, hardly worth noting. He deserved those moments of exhilaration.

I remember vividly one Sunday morning when Willie was speaking to the parishioners after mass. One of the Sisters happened to be passing by. She had gone to a earlier mass and was on her way to teach the public school students their weekly religion class. Someone generously commented on Willie's sermon as she came near them: "You missed a great sermon this morning, Sister. You should have been there." Sister graciously responded she was sorry to have missed the opportunity but had to attend mass earlier. Whether she thought it or not, she didn't mention that the assistant had given a fine sermon also.

The incident passed quickly, but something about it fixed itself in Willie's mind. He loved the Sisters and appreciated their presence in his life. He believed they might genuinely benefit from hearing sermons, even when they were not at mass. He thought about guest preachers who came occasionally to offer missions and novenas, speakers of note and prominence. He thought that when the Sisters had other things to do, they could still hear those sermons as they corrected papers, pursued routine chores or ate their meals.

The idea plagued him and the next morning he called a professional, asking about the possibility of having a speaker installed in the convent which would pick up what was being said over the microphone in the church.The consultant saw no particular problem and would be glad to come over for further planning. When he arrived, he surveyed the situation with that cool aplomb which always fascinated Willie, that technical ability which so impressed him. After preliminary examination the professional was convinced that the project could be easily accomplished — a few wires here and there, a connection, an amplifier and the magic of technology by which whatever was said in the church could be heard in the convent.

That evening Willie went to visit the Sisters to announce the exciting news. He pressed his customary three quick rings at the doorbell which announced his "official" visit. After a minimum of polite conversation he explained his plan, which he hoped would meet with approval and acceptance. He extended his remarks to include notions of being compensated by what preachers might have to say, adding to the depth of their own spirituality and being current about the directions of theology and doctrine. Willie lived in a time when the notion prevailed that Sisters were not nearly so well-educated as priests. He was practically unaware that most Sisters continued attending school in the summer and consistently pursued courses which offered updated insights into theology. As a matter of fact, most Sisters eventually came to be well-versed and up to date in what was happening in the Church, perhaps generally more so than priests.

What could the nuns say about the speakers? They certainly didn't want to seem ungrateful. They made some attempt at interest, offering noncommittal remarks such as, "That would be nice," or, "My, what will they think of next?" Willie took these observations as manifest enthusiasm and excitedly explained the system. He assured them that a switch would be installed so that if they were at prayer, say, or studying, preparing classes and such, they would be free to turn the speakers off. The Sisters, not knowing exactly what to say and being unable at the moment to consult with one another, once more offered grateful thanks. After a modicum of conversation Willie hurriedly left, happy that they approved of his plan.

When he got one of those glittering ideas, Willie pursued it relentlessly. He might have some regrets afterward and chide himself for acting so rashly, but most times he went quickly ahead. Once he fired and rehired a custodian three times in one day. Fortunately, the custodian knew him well and didn't begin removing his things until after the second time. That way it took only one trip to get them all back again. Another time he painted my entire interior a solid blue, not a stripe or block anywhere to offer contrast. It was like looking daily at a vast expanse of ocean. Fortunately again, it lasted only a little more than a year before he went back to something more sedate and peaceful.

The speaker system was in and working by the end of the week. When Sunday came, Willie couldn't wait to find out how the Sisters liked it. What could they say, except that it was just fine and they appreciated his sermon very much. I'm not at all certain this is true, but I heard later that they formed two hasty resolutions. First, they could never turn the speakers off on Sunday mornings for fear they might miss the sermon, especially Willie's. Second, they set up what might be called a "fail safe" system: one Sister was "on duty" every Sunday. Whoever it was as they rotated through the group by turns, had the responsibility to listen closely to Willie's sermon and to take the lead when he came to discuss it. She was to prepare a few statements ahead of time, leading into the subject and giving the other Sisters some clue as to the content. She should say something like, "I appreciated your reference to Our Lady of Fatima," or, "I've read that quote about St. Thomas Aquinas before." Such general observations might provide enough information to those who hadn't listened to break into the conversation and offer their own thoughts.

It all worked out well and wasn't nearly so inconvenient as some of the Sisters had thought it might be. They could go about their work and Willie, most times, informed them when something "worth hearing" was coming up. Since the speaker were installed in the community room, anyone could retire to her own cell or the chapel, out of immediate hearing. After a time no one bothered to turn off the speakers and sometimes they spoke out to no one in particular as some preacher in the church droned on with his theological disquisition. The residents grew accustomed to the sound of familiar voices and saw such minor intrusions as an acceptable addition to household circumstances. In the end, life went on, almost as it had before.

The custodians at the time, if such a word is accurate in their regard, were two local school boys, Tom and Billy, whose parents were long-time residents of the parish. They cleaned the church, took care of the yard and generally accomplished what Willie commanded. They mostly made their own schedule, both being in high school, and sometimes would come in to do their jobs quite late at night.

We were just coming into Holy Week, the last days before Easter, and Willie had told the boys to give their best efforts in cleaning up the church, emphasizing that he wanted the entire building in edifying order by Holy Saturday morning. As was their habit, both boys acquiesced readily, assuring Willie they would do their utmost, uttering those heavily used phrases which had served them in the past: "Yes, Monsignor," and, "You bet, Monsignor." They waited for him to leave, looking at each other with that pale gaze so characteristic of boys who are conspirators. They were committed enough to work, did their job, but saw for certain that there would be at least a little diversion involved.

No sense rushing in, either. There was ample time. A day or two passed before they began. There were priorities, such as professional basketball playoffs, to which both had tickets. They thought of starting their work several times, but something important always intervened — a movie they wanted to see, homework.

Finally they started one evening about nine. They attacked the job with their accustomed initial zeal, conserving their energies to endure the night. From past experience they knew the dimensions of the task at hand — sweeping, scrubbing, waxing, cleaning, polishing, a plethora of immediate duties demanding full attention. Once they began, they worked efficiently enough. I liked those boys. It made me feel a little less lonely in the night when they were there.

About midnight, perhaps one in the morning, the shadows of boredom began to lull them into something other than work. They sat down in a pew and talked a little, swirling their mops in lazy circular motions around their shoes. One of them suggested turning on the microphone and giving a sermon. The other agreed and volunteered to be first.

Feeling something of the electric call to oratory, this new born Demosthenes approached the podium with a distinct swagger. He glared peremptorily into the empty pews and began. "This is God speaking," he said with a flourish as his companion chuckled from the pew. "I'm gonna say it one more time before I turn off the lights. Shape up or pay the price. Do you have any idea how hot hell is?"

"Amen, preacher, we hear you," the other shouted enthusiastically. "Tell us one more time."

I had the firm impression that he somehow caught the fever of what was happening. He began to fantasize that the church was filled with willing listeners, leaning forward to his every word as he waxed eloquent. What he lacked in eloquence he amply compensated for in volume and acid. His imagination offered the vision of upturned faces anxious for reconciliation and pardon. His collaborator continued to offer further stimulus by encouraging him with words and phrases appropriate to fervid missionary efforts. "Amen," he shouted. "Alleluia."

All went quite well. Perhaps what the lads were doing should have offended me, all that diatribe, but it struck me as rather humorous and I thought the heavenly multitude might understand. I have no evidence to recount that they did not. Contrasted to that strident voice, there was only stillness, the usual silence of any church at midnight.

Our golden orator grew stronger and bolder, actually believing that some hidden spirit was raising him to those heights of which most lesser artists only dream. Words flowed more spontaneously now, the rise and fall of his voice giving him a convincing rhythm as he grew courageous. He began to advise and demand freely.

"I say, and remember this is God speaking, amend your old ways and think. Stop coveting your neighbor's wife. Whatever you do, remember, I am there watching you. When you slander your neighbor or bite your neighbor's back, I hear you. Beware."

The congregation of one grew thoroughly enthusiastic and entered more actively into the presentation with a staccato of "amens" and "alleluias," even an occasional "God be praised."

By now, you might have guessed that the Sisters across the way (by those speakers which had been generously installed to educate and elevate spiritually) were being roused, one by one, by the confident preaching of an expert. Not wanting to disturb the others, they crept singly into the community room to listen in fascination and terror. As each appeared, she found others there, knotted together in a small group, almost touching one another, a symbol of protection against, perhaps, the snares of the devil. Not one of them thought for a second of turning the speakers off and returning to bed. This was a case for investigation, no matter how fearful the consequences.

Who was this midnight preacher, this unbidden intruder shattering the quiet of slumber? How had he gotten into the church? How did he know about the speakers? Even as these questions were being asked his voice droned on with new threats about hell and punishment, a favorite topic of most good Christian orators. "Do you have any idea how hot hell is? Do you know how close you are to going there? Repent, before it's too late. Do you know that some of you might be there a month from now, a week?"

This last remark caused an awful shudder among some of those listeners, not from anxiety but simply from the audacity of this anonymous, arrogant voice invading their privacy. What pompous presumption to speak to these women like that! I have no way of knowing what was in the minds of those Sisters, whether one or another of them might actually have succumbed to the suggestion of this erstwhile charlatan that she could be guilty. Is it possible in these circumstances to touch some sleeping nerve, jolting us into a reluctant recollection of a former, temporary fall from virtue, long forgotten, successfully managed? I hardly think so. It is my conjecture the entire scene was simply so mysterious that it paralyzed them and demanded reasonable explanation.

Sister Agnes, the superior, suddenly had enough. Just when their smooth-tongued friend was getting to the subject of offering better example to children and not punishing them so severely, she snapped the speakers off with an expression of distaste and picked up the phone. Her fingers dialed the rectory number with a vengeance. The silence which filled the room was a startling contrast to the strange cachinnation which had voiced the demands of God. No one spoke. To at least a few of the nuns, it seemed laughable, standing quite still in their robes and nightgowns, feet bare, riveted to this circumstance that had brought them out of deep and peaceful slumber. To others, the voice had sounded vaguely familiar, similar in tone and inflection to someone they had taught in grade school at one time. But it had a gravity and accent which made them hesitate.

As the word of God was being so gloriously wrought by this unknown orator, as the Sisters stood in their ample night frocks in the dim light of the community room, as the parish at large was immersed in sweet and uninterrupted sleep, the phone jangled raucously in the rectory. Once, twice, three times and a fourth, as Sister Agnes said something to the effect that a body could die while those priests were sleeping over there. Five, six, seven times. Finally a voice, muffled and unfamiliar, sleepy and with just the slightest shade of resentment said simply. "St. Philomena's."

Without prejudice to Sister Agnes, I might relate here that she was a mildly excitable woman possessed of a firm, direct voice. She might have been described as one who was frank to the point of absolute candor, let the chips fall where they may. On this occasion when her pent-up emotion was at its absolute zenith, she shrieked into the phone without introduction or amenity, "There's a madman in the church."

Such an abrupt revelation would require some consideration, even in full daylight. Under the circumstances, in the black of earliest morning, disturbed from deepest sleep, the assistant who answered the phone was at a total loss over what had been said and who had said it. Fortunately, through habit and custom, he was able, reflexively, to beg his caller's pardon, asking for a repetition please. He was beginning to awaken and by now recognized whose voice it was which spoke so excitedly to him. Without hesitation the information was offered a second time: "There's a madman in the church."

What else to do than to offer assurance that he would investigate, now that he was up and nothing pressing until morning mass, still some hours away. Sister Agnes never identified herself. She was satisfied that she had placed the matter into someone else's hands, even though she might have questioned their competence. She hung up and instructed the Sisters to go back to bed, which they did, each with her own ruminations over this mysterious nocturnal occurrence, hoping for clarification come morning.

The assistant, more fully awake now, pondered the nature of the "madman in church." He supposed, however reluctantly, that he ought to go over, vividly remembering another time when the alarm under the chalice cabinet sounded accidentally because the door had been left slightly ajar and, encouraged by a draft, swung fully open. The alarm was wired to ring in the rectory, signaling the presence of thieves in the night, another of Willie's concessions to technology and efficient pastoral care. That sudden, cacophonous clanging had sent the assistant quickly to the church, clad in a cassock hastily thrown over his underwear. What he hadn't known was that the other assistant had preceded him by a minute or two. As he came into the north door of the sanctuary, expecting the worst, his co-worker was entering simultaneously from the south. They met with a mutual lack of recognition, in darkness and fright. They terrified each other, gasped in anguish and prepared for death. Propitiously, neither was a violent person and both refrained from inflicting physical harm. By the time light fell on the scene, an appreciable number of years was pared from their respective life spans. About that time, Willie came in, having paused to dress a little more appropriately. The three stood waiting for some explanation of their presence there, as though they had been drawn to that place by a transcendent and mysterious power, having nothing to do with ringing alarms in the middle of the night. Someone began to laugh, tentatively at first, in a dry and humorless fashion. It was catching. In an instant all three were regaled in mirth. Had someone entered at that precise moment, the Archbishop might have been forthwith informed that the priests at St. Philomena's were engaging in some ancient demonic rite whose incantations and howlings were certainly netherwordly.

The assistant hoped that this call would be fraught with similar harmless circumstances, but braced himself for the cataclysms of derangement traditionally associated with madness. Churches and such have ever offered that image of the mystical, sometimes spinning into aberrations which are personified in demonic apparitions or the curse of diabolic possession. The assistant pondered whether he was up to exorcism, should it be needed. He questioned further the advisability of entering the church, apparently under Godless siege, alone and unarmed. Should he have a gun, a strong stick, or at least some holy water?

When he left the back door of the rectory, he was encouraged by the fact that the church was fully lighted. Whoever the madman, spiritual or corporeal, he needed light for functioning. This strengthened the priest's hopeful anticipation that he was dealing with someone human. He braced himself with that line from St. Paul which assures that if God is for us who can be against us? He pondered that even demons and dark forces could never vanquish such faith. I'm not sure, because it was dark outside, but I have the distinct impression that he made the sign of the cross as he entered.

By this time Billy and Tom had exchanged places. The sermon was now winding itself around those circuitous paths so characteristic of such pursuits and was settling into a not-so-gentle discussion of the need for giving generously so that the work of God could be carried forth from this small place to the broader environs of the world. The speaker was just offering his last remonstrations to those who were stingy and tight-fisted in the Lord's regard. "As good as you are to God and His holy works, that's exactly how good God will be to you, in this life and the next. So let's keep those dollars flowing into the Lord's lap. And remember, the soul you save may be your own."

By this time the "congregation" was responding with hand clapping and cheers. It was into this that the assistant entered, befuddled and completely amazed. The next sentence of the preacher's peroration trailed off quickly, hanging there in mid-air, seeking some sort of completion, lost eternally among my pews and walls. The arpeggio of hand clapping and concelebration ceased abruptly and hung listlessly, waiting for further command. There was no sound, other than a hasty gasp and the privately heard heartbeats of those two budding disciples of Cicero.

After an entirely pregnant pause, one of the boys volunteered what he thought might be a totally reasonable greeting, "Good evening, Father." His lackluster voice held little of its previous stentorian poise. "We were just cleaning the church and were taking a break," followed by a painful silence and the ominous aura of foreboding doom.

The priest, understandably relieved that he was spared the challenge of doing battle with the dark and powerful forces of evil, praised God for generous deliverance and contrived to stanch the smile which was beginning to play at the corners of his mouth. "Did you know there is a speaker for that microphone in the convent?" he asked, assuming his fullest position of dignity and office, which was not entirely convincing since his feet were bare and his cassock, hastily donned was poorly buttoned.

"Did you know that you woke up every nun in the convent and that they think there is a madman over here ranting? And at this point I'm not too certain they aren't correct." As he said all this, he had the unfavorable impression that he had been ranting a bit himself, was getting carried away with the force of circumstances. The boys looked at him obliquely, as boys effectively do at times like these. No, that was something they didn't know and, gazing in utter amazement at each other, that communication which comes unspoken but sure from long-standing association, they both agreed that it would never in their wildest imaginings have occurred to them that a speaker should have been put in the convent. As a matter of fact, the assistant, at that ripe moment, found it rather incredible himself. For the moment he was utterly lost in wonder whether anywhere on the face of the entire earth there might be a convent which housed speakers offering every message ever spoken through a microphone in an adjacent church.

That quizzical smile began to reappear, but was shortlived as the assistant mentally reasserted that he was about serious business and of such was the kingdom of God. He offered a few further remarks, which he later judged to have been little more than platitudes, and left, buttoning his cassock which had been left unattended in the heat of pressure and fear.

He returned to the rectory, walking slowly up the stairs, wondering why he had gone to school for over twenty years to embrace his preferred vocation. In his own faulty estimate, formal education was minor, if not last on the list of those prerequisites for ministry, the kind to which he was called anyway. He had to dismiss the almost irresistible urge to call Sister Agnes to assure her that the "madman" was controlled now and that she should counsel the Sisters to sleep the rest of this night in tranquility. All was well and the spirit of evil which prowls about in dark places, seeking whom it may devour, had once more been overcome, this time by prayer and fasting, and admittedly with a minimum of heedless raving. Reason prevailed. He rolled himself under the blankets and treated his sensibilities to a reading of Gerard Manley Hopkins' exquisite poem, "Peace."

When will you ever, Peace, wild wood dove,
shy wings shut,
Your round me roaming end, and under be my boughs?

The ineffable beauty of such poetry served its intended purpose. As he lay there, it was as though his relaxed hand stretched back in time to hold firmly the stronger grasp of his dear, poetic friend, who was there on dark nights, offering soothing articulation of all he wanted to say but said so poorly. In such composure he fell quickly asleep and awakened to question whether it had all been a dream.

Morning came, inevitably, and it was the assistant's studied disposition to omit any mention of the late phone call. He held tenaciously to an early learned principle that the less one revealed to one's pastor of such things, the better off one might be. True, some revelations were unavoidable, such as who had been anointed in the middle of the night, who called for help from the local police station over a vagrant who insisted "The Monsignor" had once admonished that should he ever be in trouble, call the rectory. One had to relay pertinent information about favorite parishioners who had been suddenly stricken with life's capricious misfortunes. But some calls could be left as they were without further comment. In the experienced judgment of the assistant, this call was certainly one of those. Willie hadn't heard the phone ring and, barring communication with Sister Agnes over the events of last night, the subject might be closed and forgotten. If it were raised and the question asked why he had not been informed, the assistant was prepared to make light of it all, relate the incident in a few select sentences and offer an affected chuckle over such adolescent nonsense. He was nobly motivated, wanting to keep those two maturing preachers out of the way of Willie's righteous anger. In addition, he glimpsed an uncomfortable vision of himself and the other assistant scrubbing and waxing my interior in what might be a lengthy interim between janitors.

With the Sisters it was a different matter entirely. They were understandably agog with questions and impatiently awaited further communication. The assistant hated to disappoint them and considered fabricating some story more stimulating and intriguing than the somewhat paler truth. He would have liked, for a while anyway, to paint a picture of his struggle with the madness of diabolic intrusion, wrestling with the occult forces which are sometimes set loose at midnight in churches. He wanted, most of all, to weave a story about a priest, long dead, who sometimes inhabited churches, preaching repentance to make up for his sins of neglect in the glaring lack of preparation of his sermons while on earth. He knew he could do none of these with a composed and calm demeanor, so he simply told the insipid truth and asked for their confidence lest those juveniles be visited with wrath from on high. It was his studied conviction that if they were to be fired it ought to be for something more grand than waking a few nuns with puerile meanderings into a microphone in the middle of the night.

The assistant and the nuns shared their generous laughter, piecing together the story from its beginning by what the Sisters had heard and what had happened when the assistant had entered the church. They readily assented to maintain silence in this holiest of conspiracies. They promised to allay Sister Agnes' fears, encouraging her not to confer with Willie who was, so far, in the dark and might better be left there for the sake of all concerned. The Sisters liked the assistant and remembered nights when he came sneaking onto the back porch of the convent, somewhat occultly himself, and rang the bell to signal that it was time to drop everything and share an enticing pizza. They would then talk and laugh together, review their days and happenings since their last clandestine encounter. The Sisters accepted the assistant as genuine and were pleased to be relieved from their routine. They welcomed his company. They weren't fully aware of how they blessed his life, were a source of strength and support for him. There was agreement there, a sensitive understanding which extended to all. If at any time they were interrupted by three rings, a sure alarm that Willie had approached the front door, he was spirited quickly down the back steps and disappeared quietly into the black night. It was a sweet evasion, acceptance and love the priest needed.

Easter came gloriously that year, as it always did here, culminating in those rich ceremonies of Holy Week and the Easter Vigil. I always considered those days of special ceremony as a continuing confirmation of my existence. People came from all corners, many more than usual, packed in and offered those secret resolves so much a part of Catholic life. Some said they'd been away too long and promised to come more regularly. Others finalized their promises by confession and the pious reception of Holy Communion. Still others were content to gaze at a distance. There appeared again that yearly melange of bright dresses and ridiculously beautiful hats, serge suits and multi-colored ties. There was harmonious song and a sense of belonging to something that transcended daily routine. We were serving our purpose, the priests and I, the Sisters, the staff, the entire parish. We had come once again to that oneness which remains ideal and ethereal through most of the year, but comes to touch our souls at times to assure us that such grandeur is possible.

. I noticed, and I'm sure the Sisters and the assistant did, that Billy and Tom were present at almost every ceremony that week, near the front for a change, perhaps to hear better the words and inflection of the assistant's sermon. They beamed their approval and one gained the impression they communicated through shining eyes and benign faces what they couldn't say themselves. They might have been tempted, but left discreetly unsaid those occasional punctuations of "Amen" and "Alleluia" which could have made the sermon even more effective, if that were possible.

It was perhaps two, at most three, months later. The assistant had gone to those familiar back steps with a large pepperoni pizza, warm and appetizing. With the Sisters he shared some of the happiness of the day as they ate and talked together. When he bade them good night he slipped quietly down the stairs and ran quickly toward the church, hoping they would remain for a few minutes together in the community room. He learned later that his hope was faithfully accomplished. They were picking up glasses and moving casually about the room when suddenly they heard his familiar voice wafting electronically into the room. It stated simply, "This is God speaking." Then in strident tone he exhorted: "As good as you are to God and His holy works, that's exactly how good God will be to you in this life and in the next. So let's keep those dollars flowing into the Lord's lap. And remember, the soul you save may be your own." There followed a short pause, then an enthusiastic "Amen" and "Alleluia."

They heard that familiar click which signaled that the microphone had been disconnected. There followed a warm and affectionate silence before someone laughed, just audibly. It was another story in their lives, to be kept reverently and burnished occasionally against those days when they needed to smile and relish a well kept secret.

Chapter Twelve

THE CHURCH IS THE PEOPLE

You can't really do away with a church, short of demolishing it, taking it down brick by single brick. A church is immortal, something I've tried to say clearly in my brief expression here. Even after the structure is gone, when only the ground upon which it was built lies barren and passive, there is something there, a spirit of sorts, that keeps on living in the hearts of those who were a part of its life and history. That is because, in large part, churches gain their souls and hearts from the people who come and find home there, perhaps after years of hopeful searching. The people make the church, a simple truth but easily forgotten.

Someone once gave a sermon here about a movie he had seen concerning a parish church where the pastor suddenly died one Sunday morning while celebrating mass. The parishioners were stricken and mourned their pastor's passing, then waited patiently for the local bishop to send them another. No one came. Finally, after what seemed sufficient time, they sent a delegation to inquire if they could look for another priest. The bishop informed them, sympathetically, that no priest was available. The people simply would have to wait until he could find someone.

The people were disappointed and thought they had been neglected because their parish was out of the way. It was on an island off the coast that had only a small population of humble folks with simple needs. When the delegation returned to inform the other parishioners there was confusion and anger. Should they just wait? What were they to do in the meantime? What had the bishop said about that?

They certainly saw no reason to stay away from the church while they were without a priest. At first a few, then, gradually, all of them began quite naturally to go there each Sunday, just as they had when they had been privileged to have a pastor. They came at the same hour, said their prayers, gathered outside afterward to talk. They slowly came to sense that the parish was still there — the people, the families, those who had come every Sunday. None of them admitted it openly, but most began to discern that whatever was important in some sense remained. The priest was a part of it all, of course, something of a catalyst to set everything in motion by assuming his role in ceremonies, preaching and assisting the parish in its needs. For the first time, however, they began to think in terms of what they, themselves, had to offer. How could they care for one another's needs? How could they appreciate the gifts they possessed? What was necessary among them to bring out the good in the community?

It happened one Sunday, spontaneously, without any forethought, that someone approached the custodian who cared for the church when the pastor was alive and asked him to lead the people in prayer. It seemed appropriate enough, since he was "close to the church" and had enjoyed a more direct relationship with the priest. He was reasonably, therefore, a better person, perhaps holier in some way. The custodian demurred, protesting that it might not be respectful to take the place of the priest. The committee explained that it wasn't like asking him to do anything outside his role — just to pray a bit and maybe read the scriptures appointed for that day. After some dialogue, the custodian tentatively agreed. As a matter of fact, he found that he was pleased with their invitation and mild insistence. He rose to the occasion, feeling something positive in his response and the support of the people.

You might have guessed by now what happened. Gradually, almost imperceptibly, the substitute began to take on more and more of the offices of the pastor, but always at the request of the people and always with some protest on his part. First, they asked if he could say a few words in explanation of the scriptures, perhaps something he remembered their pastor might have expressed. Then they wanted him to talk to them about how to be better people. Finally, someone suggested they have a little bread and wine, the way they did in earlier days when they had a pastor. No one felt it would be disrespectful if their new-found "assistant" wore the vestments. After all, they were just growing old hanging there in the closet. What better way to "remember" than to use them.

And so it went, one harmless step after another. The eventual outcome of the story could have been written by just about anyone. It was a reasonable recounting of how the simple, good people of that island moved forward with their best efforts. One rather unexpected turn came in a subtle change in the attitude of the parishioners. They became convinced that if the bishop ever did determine to send another pastor to them, he would have to be at least as acceptable as their custodian, able to preach as persuasively, equally careful for the needs of the people, assisting the sick with the same gentleness. It finally became apparent that they no longer felt the great urgency for a pastor that had prompted them to visit the bishop. They never again sent another delegation to remind him of his promise to find them a shepherd.

It might be less significant to mention how the story finally ended. We can safely assume that, eventually, a priest did come. The more poignant feature of the tale, however, might be that the parish, the church and its people became willing enough to perpetuate that spirit and vital dynamic which is always there, irrespective of priests or pastors. While it was only a story, one wonders if something similar could really happen. With people of our fictional parish isolated, cut off from the mainland by an expanse of water, one can plausibly conceive that what took place there might be entirely credible. Such a condition could not prevail in a large city. People would simply go over to the neighboring parish if their pastor died and couldn't be replaced.

When Willie died, the people were stunned and confused about what might happen. Who could ever take his place? He was here for over forty years, a long time to be in one parish. Parishioners had gotten so accustomed to how he undertook his ministry, his style and manner of being a pastor, they hardly knew what to think about the priest who was coming to take his place. It certainly wasn't that they would resent a new pastor; it was just that they never thought in terms of anyone but Willie.

It is my conjecture that if Willie had been on that island out there where the people had no contact with other parishes, they would have survived. They would have assumed at least some of the duties Willie pursued so effectively. Admitting, I'm sure, they could never have functioned as well as Willie did, being even more tentative than the custodian in our story. But they would have maintained some level of health in their spiritual life. There are other stories about distant countries, China and Japan, for example, and even remote places in America where parishes were established, where priests taught, ministered and baptized and then, for some reason, left or died without being replaced. Hundreds of years passed. The people were forgotten. On returning, or upon discovering them by accident, it was a source of amazement and mystery that they still practiced their faith, retained their prayers, ceremony and ritual. There might have been some loss over the years, different words saying the same things, small differences in celebrations, even the presence of superstition and myth. But for all that, what was basic, what really counted, was still there.

What is hopefully obvious in all this is that the people of any parish are what constitute its essence. I know Willie believed this, and did, many times, assure them that they were the only reason for the existence of the parish. Except for those parishioners who came faithfully, supported what was being done, helped carry the burdens of what everyone hoped to accomplish, there was no meaning there, and no reason for a church building. Willie often began his sermons to the parishioners by assuring them that if it weren't for them, there wouldn't be a mass, no ceremonies, no need for a church building. It was the people who gave meaning to it all. He thanked them for coming, telling them that the worst condition that could befall St. Philomena's would be one in which there would be no people, an empty church on Sunday morning. It was Willie's way of saying that he appreciated every one who came with no exceptions — the regular parishioners, the occasional visitor, the interested absentee. He used to say that the priest was not nearly so important as the parishioner. He said it with such fervor that none could mistake that he truly meant it. He said that priests come and go, that he, himself, would some day not be there. It was the people who stayed on, the people to whom the parish really belonged.

I am certain that Willie was right. In my years here, somewhere over seventy now, I came to see a veritable multitude of differing individuals. They came from every disposition, espousing ideas and attitudes that cut across every kind of philosophy and idealism. The amazing phenomenon is that by far the great majority of them were extremely good and well intending. Admittedly, there were some who asked more than they gave and were a burden to the rest of the parish, petulant and angry people who thought the church ought to hold their hand through life. These were few, however, compared to the many who took their place here seriously.

In the seventy years that I lived at East Fourteenth and Detroit you could have come in on any day to find me — my sanctuary and vestibule, my pews and floors — clean and in order. Such a condition was due to the dedication and interest of a group of women who never failed to come each week, who undertook the thankless task of seeing to the maintenance and order of things. I have long been convinced that this kind of dedication and support is essential for a church and parish. It is a symbol which reaches far beyond mops and buckets, washing and cleaning. It represents, in my thinking, a sense of identity with a way of life, seeing church as home and hospitality to others who come there. That kind of devotion exists in almost any parish and deserves recognition equal to and even beyond more "heroic" kinds of missions whose objectives and impact are often more satisfying and arresting.

Most parishes have societies and organizations that interest themselves in the good of others. Here, the ever faithful St. Vincent de Paul Society functioned out of the hearts of a few compassionate men interested in the needs of others and sensitive to the exhortation of Jesus that the poor should be helped. These were mostly older men, meeting evenings to discuss matters of mercy and kind response. For those times, when there was less objective consciousness of the numbers of the ever-present poor, and before those more realistic notions of the social message of the gospel, the individual members of the St. Vincent de Paul Society represented a sincere and conscientious effort to assist the poor. They visited homes on nights they might have been with their own families. They counseled those in some stress and tried, conscientiously, to bring some good news to everyone.

There was the Legion of Mary, a prayer and action group whose goal was to make life somehow easier for those in spiritual as well as physical abjection: the sick and despondent, the fallen away, the elderly. Here one found a group that truly believed in its mission and saw membership as a holy calling.

There were women's groups, men's groups, discussion clubs, circles and societies of every description. There was something for everyone, organizations of various sorts and demands, which many, in generosity and dedication, readily accepted. The priests knew they could call on people, day or night, with requests of any description and be confident of immediate response. The people loved them and asked far less of the priests than the priests did of them. They, perhaps too readily, excused the priests' faults, revered them and taught their children to respect and love them. An enormous amount was owed to the people in the pews, that faithful contingent sometimes easily taken for granted.

The people here were the parish, the church. They gave it life, nurtured and supported it. They constituted a spirit of kindness and mutual response primary to their lives. They rose to any occasion and accepted as a group what could not be undertaken alone. They supported bazaars and sales, drives, campaigns of every sort. They passed up Sundays at home to attend the parish picnic. They eschewed evenings in easy chairs to offer support at some meeting at which decisions had already been made. They were always present, at endless sessions, lectures, missions and novenas. They belonged to deaneries and societies, made retreats and weekend cursillos, "better world" seminars — any new movement offered to them. I had the impression that they knew Willie wanted it, and that sometimes he needed them to be there more than they needed whatever it was themselves. They came and rarely complained.

Where are they all now, when I am old and only remaining here in spirit? I wish I could remember every one of them, their faces, the details of their appearance, but I can't. I can only feature them as a group, almost as though they have melded into a single good, generous, giving, always-smiling person. I remember them. I cannot forget their humor, compassion, courage, prayer, acceptance and ready support.

When people are that good, there takes place a phenomenon which cannot exist otherwise. Good is diffusive of itself, can never be contained selfishly as an exclusive possession. When people are good to one another their contribution spills over into the lives of strangers and accidental wayfarers who happen by. It is as though the good done is stored away and held in readiness for generous giving when needed.

One late night when the priests were at the end of a long day the phone rang. Such calls usually meant more than sociability or problems which could be taken care of the next day. The assistant let it ring several times, thinking someone else might be closer to the phone than he and ready to respond to an obvious need. He had been teaching that night, had an appointment afterward and was looking forward to undisturbed sleep. After the fourth ring he answered.

It was a woman, speaking in a low voice, in evident pain, catching her breath with the sound of panic. "Is this a priest?" she whispered, the tone of her voice giving way to pent up fear. "Yes, this is the priest," the assistant answered, knowing now for certain that this was more than routine.

"I'm afraid . . ." Her voice trailed off into silence. The priest broke the vacuum. "How can I help you?" Then, to reassure that he was truly interested, he said, "You needn't be afraid. Just start talking. I'll bet you'll feel better."

There are many categories of phone calls that come into rectories. Some are routine and inconsequential: What time is mass? Does the fourth grade meet for catechism this Thursday? Can you bless my medal if I come over? Others are more serious: appointments for counseling, petitions to help someone in trouble, sick calls. Death in the family is among the most demanding. It casts a pall over one's immediate circumstances by its gravity and sorrow.

Another type of phone call is even more preponderant, dreaded because of its intensity and the accompanying feeling of helplessness. As the priest listened, sensed the familiarity of the tone in this woman's voice, its anxiety and anguish, he himself became afraid.

"Can you help me, Father? I'm so afraid. I think I'm going to commit suicide. I've tried everything to stop myself, but nothing seems to help me. I'm at the end of my rope. Can you help me? Can you talk to me, give me some suggestions? Please!"

The priest froze for a moment. A tingling sensation began to prick his hands and fingers. He had that familiar feeling that he was somehow responsible now for this woman. He felt a tangible presence of guilt, which came prominently at these times, for whatever reason, as though the plight of his caller might in some way be his fault. He wondered absently what kind of depression, what insoluble problems would bring her to such a state of fear.

He hurriedly dispelled his pointless reverie and spoke earnestly to the woman. He began by gently suggesting that she come immediately for counsel, that together they might be able to find some solution and that perhaps with another opinion she would be able to see that there was some light, some hope for her. She protested that she was unable to come. She was the mother of several children, now in bed. Her husband at this minute was on his way home and she was unable to speak to him of her fears and anxiety. Perhaps if he could just talk to her, stay there on the phone for a time, the compulsion would go away.

So he did, repeating himself, offering comments he knew were of little value, encouraging her to find a time when she could come, assuring her that he would be glad to visit. She was vague in her response, said it would be impossible to set an appointment and that she thought she might be all right now.

As a final effort, not knowing what else to do, the priest asked her to call him the next morning. He wanted her to commit herself by promising that she would call. He informed her gently that if she didn't telephone, he wouldn't know what to think and would he ever know for sure what had happened? "It's only fair that you should let me know. And . . . Could you at least tell me your name?"

Even as he was saying these things, he perceived a certain lack of logic in it all. If she did commit suicide, she obviously couldn't call. If she didn't, she might simply choose to end any further conversation with him out of embarrassment and shame. Yet, he didn't know what else to say.

She promised she would call but withheld her name. They hung up. The priest had a sense of incompletion and slept fitfully through the rest of the night.

She called the next morning, apparently improved, a little chagrined over her emotion of the previous night, promising not to do it again. The priest encouraged her to seek help and invited her to come in. He wanted to know where she lived, offering the notion that she should have contact with at least one person who was familiar with her situation. But, again, she demurred, making excuses about being better now. She would work out her problems and promised that she wouldn't think of suicide again. There was nothing to do but concur, offer another word or two of advice against the too easy solution which the temptation to suicide offered. She thanked him courteously and they hung up.

It was a month, perhaps six weeks later, when she called again. It was late and he immediately recognized her strained, anxious voice. The conversation had almost identical features to the first time, the same sense of fear and helplessness against an overwhelming compulsion to end her apparently meaningless life. If there was a discernible difference it was that this time she was even more certain that she would succumb to this powerful force that would not leave her. She was intent upon a method that would take her life swiftly and without pain. She did not want to do it, but it was as though she had no control over her decision. "Could you talk to me for a little, Father?" She couldn't promise anything. She only knew that she needed someone to help her.

This time the priest was able to learn a little of this strange, periodic compulsion. It had the detail and consistency of a dependable pattern. When it first appeared, niggling itself into her mind, she was able to repulse it. But it would persist, bringing with it those convictions that her life was too burdened with the clutter of personal problems: an early marriage, children coming quickly and her husband's apparent indifference to it all. Days would pass as the temptation grew ever stronger. It angered her, depleted the energy required to say no over and over again. Gradually it wore down her forces, loomed ever larger in her imagination, bringing with it a depression which robbed her of reasonable explanations as to why she should continue to live. Finally, after days of anxious struggle, suicide seemed such a reasonable exit from her bleak life, from the daily rounds of mothering demanding children, from the tawdry setting of her home and the absence of meaningful conversation and tenderness.

This time the priest made no more progress than the first, except, perhaps, that he offered the motivation that if she could struggle through this night, if it passed, she might be able to recognize its coming the next time and take steps early to call him. Again he pleaded with her to come in to talk. Obviously there could be no harm in that and it just could be that, together, they could find a solution.

She was unable to make this commitment and thanked him for the opportunity, even if unaccepted. Perhaps she would call later for an appointment.

She did. It was in the middle of the day and he was home. She said she would like to come, that she was feeling all right at the time and agreed now that something had to be done. He was grateful and assured her that he would be there.

When she arrived she seemed rational enough and the priest remembered later his sense of amazement that people walking the streets, kneeling in pews, sitting in his classes and lectures, might be exactly as she — disturbed inside with some hidden problem, undetected by anyone, ready to hemorrhage at a moment's notice. They talked at length. She informed him that she was about to leave town. Her husband had transferred to another city. She was glad in some ways. The prospect of a different situation, perhaps some new friends, the challenge of adjustment were all attractive to her. But she was also afraid, knowing no one, of taking her fears with her to that new place. The priest talked about getting help immediately upon her arrival. He would help her find out if groups dealing with depression were available where she was going. He told her she could call him, night or day; she was certainly welcome to write; and it would be better if they kept some contact. They tried, together, to get at this strange compulsion she kept feeling, hoping to probe to its mysterious origin.

Both felt better when she left. They had taken what seemed a step toward recovery. They had added that personal regard which comes from another face and living features. Perhaps when she felt those old stirrings she might sense his presence and feel his concern for her.

She wrote after a time, informing the priest that she had gotten into a group, as he had suggested, and that it was going better now. She had made some friends and was finally able to speak to her husband a bit about her problems. She would write later, if it was all right, and hoped he would find time for a line or two if he got a chance.

He responded immediately, expressing his satisfaction that she was progressing and that he was thinking of her, praying that all would go well now. He reminded her how far she had come and that whatever appeared in the future could be met on the basis of past success. It seemed a bit shallow to him, but he didn't know what else to say.

They corresponded regularly, not frequently but consistently. She reported her progress and he responded with encouragement and support. Then her letters began to take on a different character, becoming vague and distended. They had moved again and she wanted to go to school. Sometimes he seemed to discern that she was in the same anguish as before. There was a kind of scrawling to her penmanship he had not noticed before. Her paragraphs were cumbersome and gave evidence that her thinking was unclear. He answered her letters quickly, asking if everything was all right. By this time she was in another country and it seemed possible he might lose contact with her.

He did. She stopped writing altogether and he wondered whether she was all right, whether she was still alive. The thought brought a lingering sadness. Months passed, almost a year since he had heard. He continued to sort anxiously through the mail, hoping for some word.

Then one late winter day her letter was there. She was writing, she said, after a long time, because she had been in the hospital with her problems. There were details she could not remember, lapses in her life she might never regain. She was better now, back to taking courses through a university extension and hoping to return to the United States in just a little over a year. She knew she had a long journey ahead and expressed confidence that, for the first time in her life, she felt a sense of hope about what lay ahead.

When the priest read her letter he knew, somehow, that she was beginning a new direction in her long struggle. He couldn't determine for sure what made him think it, but there was a sense of relief that assured him that she had come a long and comfortable distance from those tenuous phone calls that initiated their encounter. He thought deeply about the paths she had traversed. Perhaps he was reassured by that very distance itself, the courage it entailed. He remembered later the confident feeling he shared with her. He wrote immediately.

They corresponded again, more regularly now, but still not frequently, perhaps three or four times a year. She returned to the United States and called once when she was in a city nearby.

Because time was short and she was enroute to another state, they were unable to meet. They talked for some time on the phone and she sounded fine. She was still going to school and hoped to obtain her master's degree in Social Work.

The priest never saw her after that first brief meeting, and never spoke to her after she left except that one time on the phone. They still wrote, mostly at Christmas now, with perhaps a letter or two in between, always conscious that they would never completely sever their correspondence. It was as though there were some sacred and mystical reality they had shared which they both needed, something which offered a bond of concern pertaining to them alone. It has been over twenty-five years now and they still remain in touch. She obtained her degree and is a practicing counselor. Her children are grown, gone from home and about their own pursuits. She still lives with her husband, whom the priest never met, and still speaks positively of him and his part in her rehabilitation and growth.

Whenever the priest felt discouraged with his work, depressed over the circumstances that sometimes came unexpectedly into his life, he thought of her, of the generous gift she had been to him that late night when the phone rang. He said to himself, innumerable times: "If she could do all that, I certainly can deal with whatever little problems that come into my life." He has told her what an occasion of rare strength she remains for him, but he wonders if she really knows how her courage has buoyed and sustained him.

It is the strength of the people, just that sort of example, that gives life and vitality to the community. Paradoxically, what we do for others comes, eventually, to be a gift of precious and inestimable value in our own lives, a gift from the people, the parish out there where they walk the sometimes more difficult corridors of demand and consequence. It is the people of the parish who give the community dignity and soul, humor, a sense of belonging. How often people make us laugh and help us relish the sheer joy of life, offer us the occasion to take our strife less seriously and to widen a little our narrow vision.

A priest once told a story about a funeral at which he assisted.

He was feeling particularly melancholy that day. He had too much work, too many demands on his time, no sleep the night before, perhaps an unkind word or two from his pastor or one of the other assistants.

The burial was accompanied by a military procedure since the deceased had been a soldier in the First World War. As they gathered at the cemetery, the family was seated on small chairs at the front of the grave, the casket poised precariously above the gaping hole in the smooth ground. Soldiers were knotted at a distance, waiting for a signal from the priest that he had finished and they should undertake their last commemoration. A pervading sense of peace had entered upon the scene that spring morning. A listless breeze stirred faintly across the new grass. One heard only muffled sounds of grief emanating from the bereaved widow. There was a quiet hum of distant traffic, the intrusive reminder that life goes on even in the face of death.

A military officer read the prayer of faith that this man had served his country and that now God would take him home to the final battlefield where victory was assured and company with the heavenly battalion was his reward for devoted service. At its ending, the bugler stood ready to render taps: "Day is done . . ."

The deceased's wife heaved a sigh and leaned heavily upon the arm of her son. The sound of the officer's voice died, resonating somewhere in the distance, leaving silence and heavy hearts. The soldiers readied themselves and, at the command of their officer, pointed their polished guns toward the heavens. That process, if you are remotely familiar with it, brings its own heavy solemnity, linking religion, perhaps unreasonably, with guns and war, as though there were some special heavenly reward for soldiering and conquest. Wherever it is enacted it commands undistracted attention. There is a distinct moment of infinite and eternal silence when the single word "fire" is uttered, followed by a deafening roar which rocks across the gathered crowd. It is always shocking, no matter how many times one has witnessed it. It has that inexorable effect of deeply disturbing most who are present.

When the word was given, the soldiers triggered that blast that has been said to offer peace to the surviving members of the soldier's family, a symbol that this hero has passed on to glory and rest. The pounding sound of rifles in unison spilled over the stones to those who were buried in that small fragment of earth, a corner which harbored the death of all who fought for their country. The grieving widow could tolerate no more of it and fell into a complete faint.

At that instant, one of her younger grandsons, perhaps twelve, jumped up in a seizure of panic and shouted above the receding din, "Jesus Christ, they shot Grandma."

An older member of the family quickly grasped the boy and pulled him ungracefully back to his seat while the last two volleys at heaven were executed with precision and tight lipped decorum.

The priest stood solemnly, his pious hands wrapped peacefully around his black ritual, his cassock and stole stirring lazily in the morning breeze. When all was finished he entered his car, drove slowly from the cemetery for several blocks before turning into a side street where he stopped and gave himself over to uproarious laughter for several minutes.

The priest needed that gift. It couldn't have come at a better time. He had not anticipated anything so generous that day that would lift him from his doldrums of depression.

It is the people who make the parish. I do not recollect anyone ever actually having said it, especially those who were faithful members of the church. But I have come to the conclusion that the people are there, in their homes, in the pews and forming the long line of those who come and go, are many times beyond the priests in their goodness, their fidelity, their tolerance. We expect the priest to be loving and forgiving, the personification of all those virtues so essential to service and care. Often, however, at least some of the parishioners are more so, apparently having developed a far deeper capacity for patience, prayer and service. They are an example of what is, simply, good. And it has to be counted as extraordinary.

Permit me, please, another vignette to illustrate this goodness in the hearts of many people. One of the priests here went one evening to visit a woman in the hospital. A relative had mentioned her niece and asked if he might see her. She has suffered a debilitating stroke during her pregnancy. When he entered the hospital room, he expected to find someone in the nadir of depression, needing serious and uplifting counsel. He was wondering what he might say to offer some remote source of comfort. Contrary to his anticipation, the young woman was amazingly courageous and immediately realistic. Affected deeply, of course, by what had happened she was, nevertheless, completely willing to go on and concerned for the welfare of her baby, which wouldn't be born for several months.

They talked together for some time, she in her halting and slurred voice, paralyzed on one side, awkward and inefficient. She was optimistic, hoping to regain at least part of her loss. The doctors had told her not to expect too much. It happened that she had to transfer her dexterity and skill completely to her left side. She eventually learned to write, to manipulate such unwilling impediments as shoe laces and buttons with ease and to tolerate an entirely new method of getting along. But she did it and never complained.

When the priest left the hospital that evening, he had a nagging sense of his own limitations, wishing somehow he could tell the people something of what they continually offered to him. He was reminded of the words in the gospel which assure us that those who are last are so often first and how those who apparently die are living more fully than those who refuse to accept what is demanded of them.

There are so many who offered stimulus and inspiration to everyone here. It might have been someone who was sick and dying in an unexplainable attitude of acceptance and peace. There were people who had the heaviest of responsibilities, more than any experienced by the priests. Perhaps it was someone whose child was handicapped, a spouse whose wife or husband had been debilitated by unwanted tragedy. There were people here who cared for others, simply out of a sense of love, who had regular jobs, worked long hours and still spent time evenings assisting others, taking care of a sick person or filling in at the nursing home.

All the time these things were happening, the people felt that the priests here were the very best, excused their faults, protested that they worked too hard, that they needed a few days away. I seldom heard anyone complain about them, who said they were not doing their work, even when they weren't. The lifestyle of most of the people wasn't nearly as comfortable as that of the priests. Yet, I often heard them say they deserved the very best for all the work they were doing.

I wouldn't want to say that the priests here weren't good, hard-working and concerned for the lives of the parishioners. Obviously Willie was a totally devoted and serving priest. Most of the assistants here were, too. I simply want to make it clear that it's the people who make the parish. I loved the priests, especially Willie, whom I knew for so long and grew to understand. But I loved the people perhaps as much. I was sometimes inspired beyond telling by their courage, their dependable sense of humor, the pathos in their lives and their ability to shift and adjust to whatever came.

If there is something outstanding in my history, some excellence worth remarking, it can be described best in the people who were the very lifeblood of this parish, its substance and fiber. They are so worthy of thought, of poignant reverence. They should never be forgotten.

Chapter Thirteen

THE INEXORABLE SANDS OF TIME

Times change. It's a rule of life, a principle which can never be discarded or ignored. What was isn't any more. Who knows what will be? We flow, it seems, more quickly with age, along life's river of events.

If I have made mistakes, and I'm sure there are some, perhaps my most egregious was to think that I was not growing old. It didn't seem like it. I felt so vigorous, so full of life. Willie faithfully saw to my upkeep and repair. I seemed sturdy enough, no widening cracks in my exterior, no excessive settling of my foundation.

But I was growing old. I didn't recognize that subtle phenomenon so inevitable in every life. I think I was deluded into thinking that I was forever young because I didn't see Willie getting older, either. His quick step seemed to possess the same spring it had in the beginning. Sometimes he literally ran from one place to another. He might pass by four or five times in an hour. Next I'd hear he was at the hospital, visiting a nursing home or stopping by someone's house to chat about some project or other. He'd drop in from time to time, sitting heavily in one of the pews. Sometimes he complained about how tired he was, but I didn't really believe him. I knew that as long as he was here, as long as I could discern that spry step and strong voice, my life was secure, protected. I thought he was doing just a little normal complaining, a kind of release from tension which wasn't really serious.

Sometimes he would get sick but even that didn't bother me too much, because he bounced back so quickly and always recuperated completely. I clearly recall one occasion when he had pneumonia, undoubtedly brought on by sheer exhaustion. He sat in his room that morning in a stupor, vague and inconclusive in his conversation with the assistant. When the suggestion was made that he go to the hospital, he politely declined, but without the usual forceful rejection of the thought that he might be sick.

The assistant took the matter into his own hands, calling the hospital to prepare for his coming. Willie was too weak to dress himself and had to be helped. It was an unfamiliar scene for everyone, that kind of docility, bordering on helplessness. When the assistant brought him downstairs, Stella and Alice were waiting to greet him, offering their compassion, wringing their hands in concern and sadness. At times like these, when Willie was suffering, they became a family, looking for ways to be kind to him, remembering that, for all his usual formality and occasional bluster, he was their spiritual mentor, their father figure.

At the top of the stairs, after the assistant had led Willie from his room, it seemed he might not make it down, he was so wan and fragile. The assistant later recalled that he was hoping anxiously that he could get Willie to the hospital before he died. As they neared the lower steps where the women were waiting, Willie abruptly assumed a straighter stature, pulling himself erect and stable. His voice grew perceptibly stronger. Where just previously he had been wheezing and weaving visibly, now he spoke quite clearly, not forgetting his sickness altogether but certainly stronger than he had been a minute before.

It was that way with Willie. He had risen to a thousand occasions in his life and was at his best when challenged to respond, even though exhausted and under stress. He accepted his limitations grudgingly, and looked for ways around them. He was not an unhealthy person, even though he complained about, sometimes lamented over his ill health. He suffered the normal afflictions — headaches and those anomalous pains which beset active and intense people. He had some arthritis pains, characteristic of aging, but if these were overwhelming he certainly never indicated it. I know that at times, when he was feeling particularly poorly, he even stepped up his activity, walked more quickly, visited more and took on some of the tasks he had relinquished to the assistants. I think it was his way of waging war with his lesser self, a duel between his iron will and what he considered the forces of evil, his weaknesses. When this sort of battle was going on, most of the people around the house gave Willie wide berth, content to stand aside and watch the struggle.

On the morning in question, however, he was weaker than most people had ever seen him. As I've mentioned, it turned out that he had pneumonia, but none of those present knew this at the time. All sorts of forebodings filled their minds. The more distressed members of the group were beginning already to release him to the arms of death, fearing he had some virulent disease that would take its toll quickly and violently. Others saw at least a long stay in the hospital; no quick recovery this time. No one took the matter lightly.

Coming down the stairs, then, he surprised them by the return of some energy in his step and the strength of his voice. He spoke to them in his most patriarchal manner, complete with gestures and weighty intonation. He had something to say to everyone:

"Stella, pray for me and know that I am grateful for forty years of faithful service." This of course threw the poor woman into a paroxysm of weeping, certain that Willie was speaking his last words of comfort. He raised his hand in resistance to her, gesturing for silence, indicating the need for strength.

"Alice, what a consolation you've been, putting up with me for so long."

"Oh, Monsignor," Alice protested. "You just get over to the hospital now, and you'll be home before you know it." Then she offered that little nervous laugh which signalled that the situation wasn't at all humorous but deadly serious.

To the assistant, he left various instructions: "Call Mrs. Davenport and cancel my visit. Tell the Sisters I will be in the hospital for a few days. If important letters come, please, would you bring them over?" The assistant readily acquiesced in his usual low tone and offered words of encouragement, hoping his condition wasn't serious and assuring Willie that whatever he wanted attended to, he need only ask and it would be done.

Unless you had the good fortune of knowing Willie, you might not believe what happened next, but if you knew him you'll understand that it was entirely normal. He raised his hand as a sign that he was about to bless them. They assumed various positions of reverence, some kneeling others at least bowing. By now, it appeared that Willie's former lassitude had returned, his brief admonitions having taken their toll. He clutched the banister with his left hand and called God's blessing upon those gathered servants with his right. A renewed flush of tears and concern surfaced to the foreground of that tight circle. Willie turned to the assistant and said, simply, "We should be going." He was certainly in command.

It was a sad procession, indeed, which ushered Willie out the back door and into the waiting car. Goodbyes and well wishing once more were tenderly proffered. There was something of the color of a final procession. Under better circumstances Willie would have come in for a visit, a final prayer before departure. But this morning the car sped away, giving witness to the gravity of the circumstance.

Perhaps I understood something more of Willie that morning than I ever had before. For the first time, I began to think about growing old, becoming sick, and the inevitable prospect of death. At that moment I started to take Willie less for granted, stopped assuming blithely that he was a permanent spirit in my life, someone who would always be there. As a matter of cold fact, he wouldn't always be there. A time was coming of which I hadn't remotely dreamed, when changes would take place, new conditions would prevail. No one lives forever!

It happened, as you might guess, that Willie was hardly in the hospital door when he began to recuperate. After quickly determining that he had pneumonia, the medical professionals ordered rest and the usual application of antibiotics most often so effective. By that evening Willie was calling the rectory regularly, asking about the work there, who was taking care of various projects, and was everything getting done?

The parishioners were happy that he had recovered and was his old self again. Rosaries and novenas were offered in thanksgiving by the many who had learned every detail of Willie's bout by way of that mysterious communication that travels so quickly from person to person but can never be traced to its beginning. Flowers arrived at the rectory and a few baskets of fruit, which the assistants gratefully accepted. Stella made soups and plied Willie with liquids, garnered from a cache of home remedies which she always jealously sequestered. Alice came earlier in the day, to "catch up," her way of saying she ought to be on hand to see that he got his rest.

Within a short time, everything seemed normal again, just as it had been before Willie became sick and went to the hospital. But I knew it wasn't. From that time on there was a series of signs and happenings which indicated, however subtly, that Willie was beginning to show the effects of too much work and intensity in his life. His step became perceptibly less spry. He walked just a fraction more slowly and spoke with a hint of diminished vigor. We all knew it, but didn't want to admit what was beginning. Sometimes I heard people whisper to each other that Monsignor "looked so tired" and they wondered if anything was wrong.

"I hope he's feeling all right," someone would say, "He doesn't look a bit good."

"Well, he's working too hard. You can see it," someone else would add. "Why don't those assistants take better care of him, do some of his work for him?"

It was extremely significant to me that old Mrs. Keller died, right here in church, a few weeks later. It was after the 7:30 mass. She was just walking toward the back when she suddenly collapsed. There was an immediate clamor. Someone shouted for the assistant, who had just returned to the sacristy. He came running down the aisle but saw at first glance that she was dead. Her body was perfectly still, eyes open wide, no breathing, and her face had turned dark. The assistant returned rapidly to the front of the church to get the holy oil for anointing. As he knelt over her body to extend his hands above her, the familiar gesture of absolution, he pronounced the words of forgiveness over her lingering soul: "I absolve you of all your sins in the name of The Father and of The Son and of The Holy Spirit." I knew that Mrs. Keller didn't need absolution because she was as sinless as the day of her Baptism. Whatever she might have done was long since repaired by her life of kindness and virtue. She had died the way she would have wanted. I'm sure she approved fully.

In my time we had thousands of funerals here. They are deeply woven into the fabric of every church. Some were the last witness of the goodness and humanity of individuals who had died in mature and satisfying old age. Others were less so. Many had died prematurely, suffering and without the consolation of a long life and the accomplishments which give comfort and a sense of fulfillment. I can't clearly distinguish them all anymore. Most run together to constitute a larger whole, but some I cannot forget. Barbara was buried here years ago. She died at the age of seventeen. Cancer, that formidable word which many hear in the Dr.'s office or a hospital room after tests or surgery. She was so beautiful and young, with that kind of attraction which never serves itself but is a gift to others. She suffered a long time in the hospital, subjected to treatments and medication offered in hope of prolonging her precious life. It astonished anyone who went to visit her that she never complained, didn't call against the injustice of life and ask for fairer treatment from God. She died peacefully and the entire parish mourned her passing.

There was Billy, handicapped, deprived of those gifts others take so for granted. To walk was a herculean effort for Billy. He never ran, climbed a tree, hopped over a back fence. He painfully limped and crawled through life. He didn't speak the way others do, with sure expression, finding the proper words for description and nuance. Yet there was something so whole about him, so refreshing, that most people felt something transcendent in his presence. He didn't have much resistance and was inordinately susceptible to those quiet diseases always prowling about. One day he simply died, exhausted and depleted from too many demands on his frail body. When we buried him the church was as full as it had been on Easter or Christmas, perhaps because people understood that this was what Easter and Christmas mean — birth and death and resurrection. The priest who gave the sermon said he thought that Billy, at that precise moment, might be climbing a tree or swimming in a warm pool somewhere.

It comes to me now that many years have passed that I looked upon those funerals from a distance, impersonally, as though death were a part of life, but always the death of others, not my own. But when we buried old Mrs. Keller it was different. I kept remembering what she had said about Willie, about how she hoped he was all right. Mrs. Keller seemed perfectly "all right" when she was talking to someone a few days before in the back of the church. And now she was dead. And we were burying her. Somehow, it made me feel different inside, down deep where life pulses and generates energy to the rest of one's being.

I thought about Willie. For the first time in my long life I knew that Willie was going to die. I didn't, of course, conceive that it was going to happen the next day, or even in a month. I simply began to understand more fully that death is an integral part of life, something sure and inevitable.

A few years passed and I was happy enough with all that happened. The same routine never seemed to me to grow old or wearisome. We had Confirmations with the visit of the Archbishop. Willie loved those auspicious affairs, and felt at home with ceremonies and a bit of pomp. We had missions given by priests from some far away places who talked about their experiences to persuade the people that life without close contact with God wasn't really life at all. We had marriages and baptisms, May Crownings and colorful processions of every kind. Christmas and Easter, with all their preparations and excitement, the joy of family and seeing people who had been away for a while, were an elixir which gave happy life to everyone. Sometimes I momentarily forgot the passage of time and, in my enthusiasm, deluded myself that we would last forever. But on such occasions there was now the sobering thought, the lingering conviction, that the world was passing on, that the sweet bird of fleeting youth had flown beyond us and was off now to gather with younger companions.

When it happened, finally, I wasn't prepared. There is something about the character of life which never permits us to take in the whole of reality. Perhaps that's a blessing. We can only get hold of things a little at a time, in shadows and glimpses of a deeper essence. When someone dies, when tragedies stalk our lives, we are simply unable to think constantly, with total concentration. We must divert our thoughts to other aspects of life. What is difficult to accept, to live with, only comes gradually, perhaps never fully.

Willie had been complaining about pains in new places, and of unprecedented fatigue. Those discomforts that had once been manageable, his arthritis and insomnia, were now more insistent. Although he fought the inclination and gave himself more time to shirk whatever was intruding, he finally decided to visit a doctor. After the usual barrage of tests and experiments, the seeming endless consultation and waiting, Willie received the news that he had cancer. Surgery was ruled out because of the type and extent of the disease. He was beyond seventy years and whatever could be done would be an effort to make him comfortable and to minimize pain. What the doctor said was clear: Willie was going to die soon.

What does one do in the face of such overwhelming news? There should be some overture to cover these conditions, some way that the whole world could be present to receive the news. At first glance, it seems unfair that such weighty, life-altering information should be so simply given, there in the corner of some building by a doctor one consults only in times of sickness. The news was simply put, simply there, to be grasped however Willie might choose to accept it. Outside that small office people were walking up and down halls, busy with the press of life, life so giving and taken for granted. Beyond the windows of that fifth story cubicle, antiseptic and cool, traffic was moving at its frenetic pace, people "getting there" and leaving again, so much to do and so little time. Willie wondered how much real difference it all made.

There was little left but to go home, to take safe refuge in those familiar surroundings which had for so many years offered comfort and peace. Willie's heart was heavy.

He came over, the same way he did most days, "dropping in" before going to the rectory. He sat down heavily and mustered the courage to say what was appropriate and "right" for the occasion. He wanted to be calm, dignified. He certainly didn't want to seem unwilling to accept what was there in front of him. He had at times suspected he might be stricken by that dread disease since it had visited other members of his family. It was almost as though he had to give this cancer a personality, make it a living and conscious being, like a thief or menacing specter waiting in the wings of his life. He asked fervently that he might be strong, grateful for life and what he had been able to accomplish. Dying is far from easy, even for the strong, and Willie felt anything but strong on that quiet afternoon. He wished that death would not come slowly, in those agonizing frames of pain and terror so often associated with the disease. He struggled to straighten his body and resolutely brought his firm jaw erect, gritting in promise that whatever would be demanded of him, he would do.

He cried then, softly, with large tears, for the loss of health, for the eventual loss of life which he had loved so dearly; sweet, dynamic, active, full life, whose ending he had thought still distant, generous years away. I considered then how little real understanding we have of the short time we enjoy here. Life! its baffling mysteries. Here was a person who should have lived for much longer, whose life had been life to others, someone on whom so many depended. And now he was going to die. If there was any comfort in such ponderous thinking, it came from the conviction that Willie would always be here, offering some tangible mark of his presence, some pervading sense of his identity through the things he had accomplished. It was impossible to conceive that Willie would actually die, simply cease to be one day. I eventually came to realize that we had only to look around, at the people, the house, the church, to find that Willie was still there, visible, real. But for the moment, it was no consolation.

The days, as is their wont, turned into weeks and into months. It was Willie's studied disposition never to relinquish. He continued to say mass, visit the people and make decisions that had once been so routine and customary. The unavoidable ravages of his cancer became daily more evident, subtly diminishing his strength and resistance. He remained in bed some mornings, and went out less during the day. Finally, he succumbed to what was so absolutely demanding, the price of life, so little heeded in the beginning, so inexorable in its last word and conclusion. He could not avoid the pain and the inexpressible exhaustion which descended impersonally upon him. When he undertook even the simplest task, such as making a phone call, it drained him, stirring up feelings of utter depression which steadily lurked at the edge of his consciousness. It soon became evident to all that Willie was dying.

When someone who has been so deeply immersed in the personal life of many, it happens that those who know him take much of their own life and strength from him. When that person is at the brink of death, it appears that something in everyone is about to die with him. We identify ourselves with those who are vigorous and strong. Death does not visit the individual, rather the gathered people who have lived in long association and reciprocity with one another. The death of one signals the demise and diminishment of all.

It was certainly that way with Willie. A pall of disbelief and sadness descended on our parish. Everyone wanted to see Willie one more time, sit for a few minutes with him, ask him once again for his presence in their lives. It was, of course, impossible and that person who, during his long life, had never refused service or response to anyone found this agony perhaps more difficult than physical pain and the prospect of death. People left messages which were read to him when he was feeling able enough to receive them. He wept over his inability to see his friends. The sure realization that he would never talk to most of them again brought an added sadness, as though he were abandoning the very ones who had sustained him for so long.

One of his former assistants came to visit, wanting to maintain the contact established when Willie was healthier. The premonition that death was very near had taken hold. Somewhat compulsively he left his work on a Sunday afternoon and drove seventy miles to Denver to visit Willie. He knew, somehow, that it would be the last time. The assistant had passed long years in the parish, happy enough but with that usual toll of adjustment and pain that are constituents of any relationship.

To intimate that their mutual communion was always cordial and unfractured would be to miss the truth and the point as well. The assistant and Willie were obviously different in their ministry and assessment of what was important to each. Their years together suffered the usual tension present in most relationships and perhaps more prominent in the case of pastors and assistants. They had never really fought, never exchanged those normal diatribes of injury and invective all too often shared by those who work together closely. The assistant liked to think that he was principally responsible for a kind of cool peace which had prevailed at times of belligerence and ill humor. Conversely, Willie thought that they had done as well as they had together because of his own tolerance and the more moderate expectations he had placed on this overly sensitive and somewhat insecure assistant.

For the most part, their continuing acceptance of each other was admirable. Sometimes months passed without an eruption of anger and contentious self defense. But, for whatever mysteries of life which contribute to one's imperfection and weakness, peace would be sometimes unwittingly interrupted by what, afterward, always seemed some insignificant and minuscule circumstance. It was as though larger hurts had been stored for future reference, a day when a coalescence of unattended feeling burst into the flames of accusation and disregard. Then, and always regretfully in retrospect, they said and did what was beneath their respective better selves. They both tried to accomplish something positive out of every harmful encounter, but their individual natures, limited as they were, grew brittle again and eventually precipitated the incompatibility perhaps normal to any close relationship. Because they had spent years together, some lasting hurt had been rendered where charity should have prevailed.

With this history the assistant came on that January afternoon into the presence of sick, feeble Willie. The ominous intrusion of impending death often neutralizes much of what was formerly perceived as gravely important. Willie greeted the assistant with cordial animation and welcome. The assistant felt comfortable and sat quietly while Willie talked about himself, revealing his fear and the intuition of so little time remaining. They exchanged thoughts about ministry. Willie asked about the assistant's work and offered concerned counsel about not working too hard over the demands which parishioners sometimes place upon willing priests.

Time passed gracefully. There was no niggling compulsion on the assistant's part to finish the visit, as though he were simply on an errand of duty. At one point Willie asked if the assistant could lift him a little, help him sit more erect for a time. As the assistant complied, taking Willie into his arms and raising him carefully, it struck him that, in all the years they had lived together, they had never been as physically close as at this moment. To his recollection, they shook hands occasionally, but never embraced, never put an arm or hand around the other's shoulder in a gesture of affection and warmth. The assistant felt a poignant sadness at such an irretrievable loss and unconsciously tightened his grip on Willie's shoulder.

At that moment, caught somehow in the flux of so much which moves too quickly, and now stilled for an imperceptible instant, all that tension, the hurts in their history, the unhealed wounds which lingered in the unforgotten past, paled to insignificance and lost their former sharp injury. Willie began to weep. One might have later analyzed such a reaction as due to weakness and distended emotion. But the assistant knew that life comes to a point of equalization where what once seemed grave becomes exceedingly less so, what was estimated as highly consequential assumes a far more reasonable character. It was a moment of reconciliation and peace, of forgiveness and the deep need to say that what had passed between them could be relinquished. The tight fist of personal defense could release its tenacious grip and those old tensions could be dissolved. It was a marvelous instant. Some might have said it was a miracle.

There were no words, no exchange of mutual pleading for forgiveness. It would have been inappropriate. They simply sat together, the assistant gently supporting Willie's back and shoulders. They both wept for a time, without embarrassment or drama, a gift which the more basic realities of life freely bring.

Shadows of late afternoon crept into the room. The assistant offered his assurance of prayers and warm thoughts, promising Willie that he'd return soon so that they could talk again. In his heart he knew it was the last time he would see Willie alive. He acknowledged that their visit had been a welcome gift and wanted to say, had he not said it before, that he was grateful for what Willie had taught him. Willie, in his turn, thanked the assistant for having come, for having taken the time. He said that he liked to think that every one of his assistants had taught him something, had given a gift. He assured this one that there was much in his heart which had come from his hands. He cherished it all.

The assistant left quietly, spoke a little to the people downstairs and went out into the last light of that winter afternoon. The sharp air quickened his step. He was filled with reverie and a sense of how many times he had left that rectory, walking or running to the next errand, to the duty that lay ahead. They perhaps numbered in the thousands. It occurred to him that he was leaving it all for the last time. He turned to look at the house, the church rising above the other buildings in the area. He paused for the length of a breath or two, turned again and walked more slowly toward the street. Stopping once more, he came inside to kneel at the back pew. His thoughts centered around the meaning of it all, questions which might forever remain unanswered, a flicker of light when one understands a little, yet so much remained in those obscure realms that must be accepted without clear discernment.

Willie died two days later. That powerful body which had housed the once young and yearning spirit, which hoped to bring a new gift to the world, was dead. He breathed his last breath sometime in early morning. It was a passing which marked the end of what had begun long before but would continue until the last person on earth who knew Willie joined him in the partnership of death. What Willie had done would not end but would be passed along from hand to hand in generations to come, unceasing, growing and multiplying in those who would preserve what was best in him.

A part of me died with him. Perhaps it was the best part, what he had given me, his concern for a place where people could be welcome, to pray, the house of God, to be at peace. Ours was a unity of purpose, an understanding of the meaning of "Church," "St. Philomena's," words which had taken on a tenor unmistakable to those who heard them. It could not have been spoken without the inclusion of Willie. It was unthinkable that anyone could say, "St. Philomena's" without saying, at the same time, "Willie," "The Pastor," the shepherd who took us into his care.

I would miss him. He knew every brick of me, every board and rafter, joint and studding, the walls and corners, wrapped round with the plaster and facade of a dozen trimmings, the paint over paint of years of refurbishing, the pews and floor, the lofts and attics, the dug out hollow of my lower life where the furnace growled and gave off the assurance of warmth and welcome. He had come a thousand times, walking the length of my center aisle to relish the presence of my life in his own. We were holy partners, bidding for the best in the life of those who came, offering courage to come apart and rest a while, to be strengthened for what lay ahead. My spirit was molded by his presence. Even though I stood there on the morning of Willie's death, appearing for all intent exactly the way I had the night before, something was gone now, never to be replaced or continued. Something in me had died.

There was in the days to come a character of numbness which overtakes those who mourn and lament the loss of someone from their midst. It seemed to me that people whispered and exchanged hushed remarks, as though Willie might still be listening, as though he might be wanting to say something himself. We were caught in the dream of recollection, talking readily about what he did, things he had said. I thought of so much, perhaps because I missed him and wanted to bring something of his presence to mind. I thought of sermons he had given, what he had said, his mannerisms and features. I thought of the time he walked into the middle of mass with a small radio in his hand. It was during the World Series. I'm sure Willie didn't care who was playing but was caught up in a flush of enthusiasm for the very gift of life at that compulsive moment. He boldly announced to the congregation, just after communion, that Pittsburgh was leading four to one. I thought of what he'd said to children at mass on First Fridays, stopping often to explain parts of the ceremony. It would have made popes roll over in their graves, but it was Willie and it somehow fit his personality without irreverence or offense. I thought of how he loved the people, served them, was a giving pastor. I thought of how Willie was dead, but somehow still there, walking in and out. Sometimes I thought I heard his voice, clear and strong again, saying something familiar: "God save us, Mamie, you look better than you have in thirty years."

Late at night, when the furnace was sleeping and only the vigil lights were blinking faintly, when the pigeons which came to roost had ceased their mournful call, I imagined I could hear his unmistakable footsteps, his voice at the rectory saying, "Good Night." It comforted me some.

Willie was buried at the Cathedral. Everyone knew so many people would come they'd never accommodate them all here. Stella said it was a "beautiful" ceremony, that the bishop had good things to say about Willie. The church was full, overflowing with Willie's friends. Some wept and said they couldn't imagine he was dead. He'd been here almost forty-five years. They lowered his body into the earth with the usual prayers said at a funeral. "May the angels lead you to paradise and may the heavenly choirs come to welcome you." I wonder what Willie thought of it all? I have the impression he is at home. I wonder if they've asked him to preach yet?

Life went on here, not the same but with its own shades of meaning and purpose. New pastors came, several of them, good and well intentioned. They took care of me but, obviously, a part of me was missing, lost among those events which had taken place so long ago. The people came. We said our prayers and marched into a new era which would have left Willie puzzled and confused: the Vatican Council with its documents and letters, liturgical reform, congregational singing, the "age of the lay person," parish councils, corporate decision making and a multitude of other changes which transformed the Church completely. But we fared well, were used to taking our part, and adjusted. Actually, the people here liked what was happening, most of them anyway. Sometimes we heard about priests and Sisters who were leaving, some from this very parish. But we took it in stride and talked of a better Church, looking forward to what was to come.

Rumors flew from time to time about merging with another parish, making St. Philomena's a kind of satellite church. They talked of changing my name and eventually did, but it didn't hurt me, mostly because all but a few officials continued to call me St. Philomena's anyway. They said that fewer people were going to church in this area and that we didn't need so many churches as in the old days.

We moved along with it all and didn't complain much. As long as the people knew they had a place to come on Sunday, their home, they were happy enough.

Finally, the day came when they said I would have to be torn down, dismantled, if that's the right term. There were words and phrases having to do with "making way for progress" and "moving ahead." It was impossible for me to believe. I thought of Willie. He would have taken it hardest of all. I was glad he was with the "heavenly choir" and knew that in those places there was more perfect understanding.

Many of the old time faithful parishioners were angry, desolate with the prospect that I was to be destroyed. They tried to stay the decision, but it had already been made. There was, apparently, nothing anyone could do. They staged some protests, asked for dialogue with church authorities, but very little came of it. I wanted to maintain some dignity and refused to lose my composure. I was determined to stand erect and strong to the very last. I wanted to console myself that history was in the making, that I was clearing the path for what was to replace me, something better, modern, a contribution to the lives of many. But I was only deluding myself, depressed and saddened that the passage of time had finally caught up to me and demanded recompense for so much that had been freely given. I was to be destroyed.

I cannot pretend to have a faithful recollection of everything that took place in those ensuing sad days. It is all a blur to me now and nothing is completely clear until the morning of my "death." They — that anonymous grouping of disinterested workers and directors — had brought in sundry machines and equipment for the purpose with trucks and derricks of frightening dimensions. A long crane hovered above my roof and towers. A gathered cluster of spectators stood to the side gazing diffidently at my helpless predicament. I remember that the sun was shining brightly in the morning sky, giving courage to the workers. It was a day for accomplishment.

I watched with the intense interest of one who is present at a sentencing and pronounced guilty. Of what? I did not know. I was surrounded by those who looked upon me with a range of attitudes from studied detachment to close, personal involvement. I had the feeling that there were some present who were weeping, marking the sad passing of a living reality with which they had identified and found companionship for a lifetime. Perhaps there were some there who had been baptized at my door. There certainly were people within short distances who had watched some seventy years before as other workers of a less sophisticated age had carefully laid my foundation, fashioned row upon row of those well selected tan bricks which stood so strong through seventy winters and bore the heat of an equal number of summers.

I stiffened as the derrick sprang into action, coughing the foreboding sounds of destruction. I watched in anguish as the gigantic steel ball swung slowly up and over my roof, reached the limit of its tether, balancing at the very zenith of that great crane which protruded arrogantly over the top of my towers. For a fleeting moment those seventy years stretched lucidly before me, gathering a force of comfort and peace, soothing in the presence of that prophetic round weapon. I caught the distinct vibration of its indifference before it suddenly released and gained the terrific momentum of descent toward my innocent structure.

The round, shining steel ball had suddenly achieved its consummate essence, its meaning and singular purpose. Its fierce plunge became resistless, a force unto itself, uncontrolled with awful destiny. When it reached my roof, it penetrated swiftly, almost gracefully, and disappeared within. There was a deceiving instant of silence, an eternity of still anticipation before my frame exploded, spewing debris and random material about the yard. The roar of impact was like a cacophonous shriek, a splintering wail for what could never be again. The church, I, my existence and life, had died.

I searched within myself for some mysterious rationale to justify destruction in the name of progress. You can't save everything, preserve it forever. Buildings grow old, obsolete, out of mode. Bricks and boards can be replaced, but not the living. All that emotion, the sorrow, the joy, the rise and fall of laughter and tears, so characteristic of any "home;" the love which makes the life of bricks and walls significant and true.

The ball had risen again, scaling the height of that blue morning sky and belligerently intruded my reverie, crashing a second time. And I died again.

It took a mere two days. Walls and roof fell, gables tottered, careening drunkenly to the ground below. Trucks and dozers pushed and heaved as they crawled listlessly over my blood and bone. The plot where I had stood was smoothed over, planed and folded back as though I had never been. The guise of circumstances gave duplicitous testimony that I hadn't existed, had been only a figment, a dream gone back to rest.

It is one of life's deeply consoling gifts that life is limitless and cannot be circumscribed, made to remain within fixed limits. As I said long ago, it is the spirit which retains persuasion. You can take down a wall, but never the impetus and soul required to put it there. You can remove a structure, but never the life within. God knows, we need that. The world would only be dull and lifeless without it. It gives me comfort, the solace of knowing that some things last forever. It is a joyful thought that I am still here, St. Philomena's Church, built on the rock of Peter back in 1911, taking my place still among those who have gone before and are yet to come.

Sometimes, when the evening sun is gently shedding its last rays through the neighborhood trees; sometimes in pale winter's light, the whole of Detroit Street seems to catch an aura of bright life, the last strong irridescences of glory before evening repose. I'm glad to be a part of that and find it impossible to imagine the neighborhood without my being there, those tan bricks and tall towers which most people thought would last forever. As a matter of fact, I do. Stop for a minute, use your imagination and you can see me there, quiet, unobtrusive, the way a church should be. If you listen, strain just a little, you can hear my voice: "Come in. Rest. And be at home."

Chapter Fourteen

THE REQUIEM OF A CITY CHURCH

What is it like to be a church for over seventy years? Much the same, I'd conjecture, as being a person, a living composite of body and soul. There are feelings and thoughts which become so much a part of oneself they defy separation and independent existence.

If I were asked to describe myself, I would want to begin with what took place within, deep down, inside; every prayer and ceremony, every word whispered in confidence inside my walls and windows. I would have to say that the life blood flowing in my veins, coursing through my bricks and timbers, the pews and furnishings, is composed of incense and a million chantings and imprecations for the grace of a good life, for virtue where it is most needed, for a happy death and heaven to follow.

I am not a sterile church, lifeless, nondescript bricks and walls. I am living, a breathing being, sustained and ensouled by the breath and life of the people who came here, who walked in and left something of their vitality and nurture. Their soul is mine now, immortal and eternally remembered. What they did and said here became part of me. And what I was, a church, the house of God's people, is remembered now in them, so that, by such an infusion, we are inseparable, a transcending spirit which created in us something more than we could have ever been individually.

How can anyone say I have gone, evanesced into the folds of time to be no more? If I am in the minds and hearts of those who came here, I am still living. I have not died, not so long as there is one member left to tell my story. Not so long as there is one word which gives utterance to my long journey.

How can it be otherwise: Does death ever really prevail where life has existed and been shared around the circle of friends and family? Does the spirit cease to be when one member of the community ascends to the level of memory to be sustained and passed on by the other partners in the group? For my part, I am surely there, the same as always. I have transformed now, into the minds of those who knew me, who have me inside for keeping and memory. I continue to be what they are. Their life is mine. My life continues as they pass life on to those who come after. I am confident that when the present course of life ends, I will be there, called up with the rest, somehow enlarged, to embrace every person who stood or knelt in prayer in the eternal embrace of my loving arms. It is the gift which was given to me on that day when Michael turned the first spade in that fertile soil which gave rise to my life and growth. It is the blessing which Willie continued to nourish by care and love, his recognition that I was much more than dead stone. There will ever be evidence of this in that long line of people, faithful and ardent friends, who graced my house with their presence, coming to discover something they could never find in other places, no matter the elegance or stature of those other surroundings.

I am here because the people have been here, people with their old, gnarled hands and wrinkled, timeless faces upturned in silent prayer, convinced that there is more to life than the immediate present. I remain here in the hearts of the young, so bold and sometimes heedless, but born with the seeds of hope and comfort that God comes always in those strange ways which take a lifetime to understand. I am here for all those who come eventually in separation and reconciliation to sit and ponder the meaning of their lives, who go away and come back again to sit in consolation and peace.

Please do not tell me I am a church no more, that I am dead. I have opened my doors numberless times to those crying infants who did not yet know the significance of their weeping, a clamor for justice, peace, satisfaction. I heard them and gave hope to their parents who stood in commitment to put faith into the hearts of their children. "Ego te baptizo . . . ," I baptize you into God's family, into its yearnings and hopes. I baptize you, give you more than you will give, the gift of life, eternally, into the tradition of a billion forbears who have gone before you that you might come to this place.

I echo the cries and longing of every voice which has risen inside these happy precincts. I have given life out of the abundance within me still.

I have witnessed the troth of that endless circle of lovers who have come to stand before the people here to testify that life can be better for the diffusion of love. It is I who have housed that hope for happiness beating within the secret heart, stretching onward through life into eternity. I have listened and healed those who have returned in disappointment and hurt, seeking yet for love. I have celebrated with those who stand in joy for unions which have endured through the worst and the best of times. I have blessed and honored the good in their lives and loves, linking their union in God.

I am a church and beyond that, transcending a simple building, mute and cast forever in stone. I am that voice which rises out of the past and gives meaning to what is present and yet to come. I am indistinguishable, inextricably interwoven into every person who aspires and dreams.

I was not buried with the dead. I have remained to give memory and evidence to their lives. There is no beginning or end in me. What does it matter that one day they began to lay the foundation and bricks of me, set in the roof and shingles? I was there before, brother and sister of every church which has been from the beginning. If they have taken me down, dismantled my bricks and towers, I remain the substance of what all churches have been. We are one structure, the symbol of that transcending connection to the deepest part of every being. We are one: one building, one set of walls and windows, welcoming the people in. We are the house of God's people.

There is an endless moving line of numberless individuals rising out of time who continue to come in, who will come in now to other churches, other parts of me, where I have gone to take rest and refurbish my spirit. There is that multitude of persons who have taken me in, knowing that it is not a lifeless structure they have sought, but a vital and moving force of creation and life.

I have no regrets, nothing which weighs heavily on my heart. If it seems I have been rudely relegated to the annals of history, discarded in the minds of some, I am hallowed by many, gently garnered in the memories of countless people who know me. One day of life would be enough, one hour, if it were filled with something memorable, a Palm Sunday procession, the ritual of midnight mass, an early morning visitor who drops in to pray, a solemn funeral of an old and revered parishioner, more joyful than sad because of what that person left behind.

I had more than an hour, more than a day. I was given seventy-five years of continuing and consoling activity; years of the best of people's lives. There is so much there. With a moment's reflection I can smile and remember. I can shed those sad tears over what was good and has passed now. I couldn't have asked for more.

There is nothing I haven't experienced, nothing I've wanted. I have watched and been a part of it all, undeserving as I might have been. What circumstances were at work to bring it all about? What independent lines of intention came together to bring me into being on a given plot of ground at a specific time in history? It seems less important than to accept the joyful truth that I was here and felt the pulse of it all and could tell about it.

And now, I'm only asking you to remember. If you come by my corner, you'll see an unoccupied, lonely piece of ground, a few weeds, bits of litter, ever present evidence of civilization. If you stop for a moment and dream a little, you'll be able to see my walls there, the towers rising above those high walnut doors bidding entry to the silence and peace within. If you approach you'll see a crowd so dense and concentrated you'll have to imagine that my small structure has been enlarged to accommodate a great throng. Everyone is still there — the priest from the beginning to the end, Willie directing and officiating, only this time more benign and cordial than ever. That connecting span of assistants will be there, all somehow at harmony and peace; the Sisters, gentle and strong women who wait for us to recognize their generous gift to the parish, undemanding, selfless. And the people, the people. The giving, kind, forgiving, sensitive, virtuous, loving, forbearing, compassionate, sympathetic people, without whom a church would merely be a bare and sterile building. The people who give life and meaning to the inside, down deep, part of me, who leave their prints on my floors, the pews and the kneelers; whose voices ring and whisper in tentative song, in joy and the quiet of devotion.

Somehow it is different now. Everyone is there. Marigold has come and been welcome. She has brought her friends. I see Harvard Brophy sitting beside his wife and children. They are holding hands. Stella, Alice and Ruth are kneeling together, regaling each other with recollections of happy times. I see Mamie sitting with old Mrs. Keller who died long ago at the 7:30 mass. Tom and Billy are beside them, grown now but still sharing their adolescent secrets.

You are there, with your family, your friends of long association. You have come with all those who are named and remembered as parishioners. You are kneeling and standing to the tempo and harmony of what it means to be at home.

Willie is smiling broadly over it all, passing among his beloved people. You can see those familiar tears surface to his glistening eyes, and the characteristic set of his jaw to ward off that unwanted emotion. He is realizing that it matters little now. He is home, home with us all, where he can weep for the joy of life with us, for the fullness which comes to those who serve, who honor the lives of others. We can say to him now that his work was well done. And he can weep openly, for the first time that we have seen, with large tears, as though pent up too long, released finally, easily, coursing down his cheeks to fall unashamedly to the floor.

Faint strains of music swell to more audible levels, growing to a crescendo of finality. No sadness here, where every tear is wiped away. There is no hurry, no time to leave. That euphoric thread of melody gives rise to song in the heart of every person here. They sing in harmony and splendor: "Dona nobis requiem." Give us rest. And rest has come.

Afterwords

St. Philomena's Church was indeed torn down, leveled to apparent non existence in June of 1984. In just a few days after its de-construction, passers by might have assumed that it had never been. We are so clever at "restoring" sites and such to their natural setting. What was an imposing structure was now once more a vacant lot. In just a few months, weeds began to appear, a merciful covering over the injured and scarred soil. They offered the illusion that the land had lain untouched, as though it had always been just ground and never anything else.

The original projection, to build an apartment for senior retirees of upper level income, was somehow abandoned. Perhaps unfeasability and lack of enthusiastic response contributed as much as anything to a more realistic review. For all that, St. Philomena's could not be brought back, restored to its former nobility and stature. History doesn't offer that gracious sort of redress. We are left to do our best under trying circumstances, remember, and not forget.

Eventually a new direction began to evolve. Was it possible to more realistically use the property for moderate income tenants? Wouldn't that be much more in keeping with the humble beginnings and modest life of this simple church and parish? Could the message of goodness and care still be conveyed in a place where the church had been?

Construction of a low cost apartment complex was begun in August, 1989. The building has now been completed. To the uninformed viewer, everything seems normal and in its place. Let it be, this new structure, this new building, replacing what the older one was. To those who know, who came on countless Sunday mornings and other days, it is a consolation, that not all has gone, that it is still there, transformed, renewed. Let it be.